THE FATHERS
WITHOUT THEOLOGY

THE FATHERS
WITHOUT THEOLOGY

by

MARJORIE STRACHEY

NEW YORK

GEORGE BRAZILLER, INC.

1958

LIBRARY OF CONGRESS CATALOG CARD NUMBER: 58-6625

PRINTED IN THE UNITED STATES OF AMERICA

André Gide used to tell the following story of Voltaire. A young man who wished to consult him was shown into his library to wait. Seeing a long row of the works of the Church Fathers on the shelves, he pulled one or two down and found the margins covered with annotations. When Voltaire made his appearance his visitor greeted him with some astonishment.

"Comment, Monsieur," he said, " vous lisez les pères de l'église?"

"Ah," replied Voltaire grimly. "Ils me le payeront."

ACKNOWLEDGEMENTS

Quotations are included from :

Eusebius : Ecclesiastical History, translated by Kitsopp Lake, by kind permission of the Loeb Classical Library.

The Shepherd of Hermas, translated by C. Taylor, by kind permission of the Society for Promoting Christian Knowledge.

The Apocryphal New Testament by M. R. James, by arrangement with the Clarendon Press.

To
J. S. B.

INTRODUCTION

What do we mean by *the Fathers?* By common usage the term is applied to early writers on the Christian religion, not, of course, including those whose works are enshrined in the New Testament. These writers form a vast and heterogeneous class. They include orthodox saints, known at least by name to everyone, such as Jerome (342–420), Chrysostom (*c.* 347–407), Augustine (379–430); heretics, such as Origen (185–254) and Pelagius (fifth century); and many anonymous writers such as the authors of the edifying *Epistle to Diognetus* (*c.* 150) and the less edifying apocryphal Gospels, Acts and Epistles, for the most part gravely heretical, but not the less worthy of study.

These writings form an immense and somewhat indigestible mass. Of vital interest to the professional theologian, they are apt to throw the uninitiated layman, should he attempt to penetrate their mysteries, into an abyss of boredom and metaphysics. Yet buried here and there lie many curious gems which it may be worth while to extract and examine. There is much that is instructive, much that is surprising and entertaining. Leaving aside theology for the theologians—or at least giving only so much as to make the rest comprehensible—this book is presented to the ordinary reader, in the hope that it will afford him some new light on early Christianity and perhaps some unexpected amusement.

The book covers the period from the beginnings of Christianity to the Nicene Council 325. It includes practically all the writers of the second and third centuries, though some, known only by fragments, or interesting only for their theological disquisitions, have been omitted. They are discussed as far as possible in chronological order and a chronological table will be found on p. 233.

CONTENTS

11

I

The Apostolic Fathers

THE earliest of our writers are known as the Apostolic Fathers, because it is claimed that they were in some way or other connected with the apostles themselves. As is to be expected with the infant church their works are very varied in character and outlook, and not all of them were entirely approved in later ages.

Clement of Rome

The first of the Apostolic writings—the only one that is generally believed to belong to the first century—is known as the *First Epistle of Clement to the Corinthians.* This letter begins, "The Church of God which sojourns in Rome to the Church of God which sojourns in Corinth." The author nowhere names himself, and it is by the widely supported tradition of the second century that it is ascribed to Clement, one of the first bishops of Rome. The purport of the letter is to put an end to the disputes and irregularities which appear to have been rending the Church of Corinth, giving it a bad reputation in its heathen surroundings. The writer apologises for having delayed to write—the delay is due, he says, to "the sudden and repeated calamities and misfortunes that have befallen" the Church of Rome. This is in all probability an allusion to the persecution of the Christians, instituted by the Emperor Domitian in A.D. 95. We hear further of the martyrdom of St. Paul, "who taught righteousness unto the whole world and reached the farthest bounds of the West." This perhaps means Spain, and is the source of the tradition that St. Paul visited and preached in the Iberian peninsula. The martyrdom of St. Peter is also mentioned, though we are not told that it took place in Rome, nor is it stated that St. Peter went there.

After pointing out the importance of the Christian virtues, among which he gives a high place to *orderliness*, the writer goes on to speak of the benefits which God has bestowed on his people. Among these benefits He has promised us the Resurrection of the Body, of which there are many signs in the world around us.

"Day and night show us the resurrection. Night falls asleep and day arises; day departs and night comes on. Observe the fruits of the earth. . . . The sower goes forth and casts his seeds into the earth, dry and decayed. Then the Lord's providence raises them up and they increase many times and bear fruit.

"Let us consider the marvellous sign which is seen in the regions of the Eastern lands, that is the countries round about Arabia. There is a bird, named the phoenix. This is the only one of its kind, and lives for five hundred years. When it has reached the time it should die it makes for itself a nest of frankincense and myrrh and other spices, into which it enters, and so dies. But, as the flesh rots a certain worm is engendered, which is nurtured from the moisture of the dead creature, and puts forth wings. Then, when it is grown strong, it takes up the nest where the bones of its parent lie, and carries them off, journeying from Arabia to Egypt, to the place called Heliopolis, the City of the Sun. And flying by day, in the sight of everyone, it places the bones on the altar of the Sun and then hastens back to its former abode. And when the priests examine their records, they find that all this happens exactly at the moment when the five hundredth year is completed."

The connection between the story of the phoenix and the resurrection of the body does not seem quite clear. But it is a pleasant tale, and we will hope that it helped to convince the Corinthians that they were wrong to be disorderly, and that after receiving Clement's epistle they reformed their ways.

* * * * *

The earliest manuscript copy of the New Testament—the Sinaitic MS. of the fourth century—contains in addition to our New Testament, two early Christian writings—*The Epistle of Barnabas* and *The Shepherd of Hermas*—both of which were considered as inspired writings by the early Church, but were later dropped from the canon. Their authors and dates of composition are unknown, but it is generally agreed that they must have been written before A.D. 150. A third book is connected with them. It is known as *The Didache*, or the Teaching of the Twelve Apostles. These three books are no doubt connected in some way, but in *what* way is a puzzle, much disputed over by the learned. The problem, however, is not one into which we need enter here.

The Shepherd of Hermas

The Shepherd of Hermas is unique among early Christian works, and has been compared with *The Pilgrim's Progress* and the *Divine Comedy*, though unfortunately it contains not a spark of the genius of Bunyan, much less of Dante. It is nevertheless an interesting production which merits attention.

It purports to be a record of the experiences of one Hermas, who himself tells the story. It is written in an allusive style, from which we may piece together much that concerns the life and character of Hermas.

He seems to have been born in Arcadia. He was perhaps exposed as an infant and picked up by a slave dealer as a speculation; in any case he was bred up to be a slave, and sold to Rhoda, a lady of Rome. He married and had several children, but his married life was not satisfactory. His wife was a scold and a back-biter, his children disobedient and reckless in wickedness. Hermas himself was to blame for this, for he had spoilt them and neglected them, from being preoccupied with his worldly affairs. He was however in many ways an amiable character—patient, calm, chaste and simple-hearted, always cheerful and merry.

He was freed by Rhoda and acquired a small property which he farmed himself. After many years he met his former mistress again and began to love her as a sister. One day he saw her bathing in the Tiber. He held out his hand to her, and helped her out of the water. Gazing at her beauty, and remembering her kindness towards him, he thought to himself, "How delightful it would be if I had a wife like her—so lovely in appearance and so virtuous in character." But this was only a passing thought, and he did not dwell on it.

After Rhoda's death he was walking on the road to Cumae, the ancient abode of the Sibyl, and being tired he lay down by the roadside and fell asleep. In his sleep he had a vision. It seemed to him that a spirit carried him to a desert region, pathless, rugged, and broken up by water courses. He crossed a river and coming to level country knelt down and prayed. As he prayed the heavens opened and Rhoda appeared to him. She greeted him by name. Amazed, he asked her why she was there.

"I was taken up," she replied, "to reprove your sins before the Lord"; and on Hermas questioning her further, "God," she said, "is angry with you on account of your sins against me."

Hermas was horrified and indignant.

"Against you!" he cried. "How did I ever sin against you? Did I ever speak an unseemly word to you? Did I not always regard you as a goddess, as slaves should regard their owners? Did I not reverence you as a sister? Why, lady, do you falsely accuse me of wickedness and uncleanness?"

Rhoda smiled. "The desire of evil entered your heart," she said, "and that is a great sin even if no deed follows. They who entertain evil purposes and set their affections on this world, boasting of their riches, forget the world to come. But pray to God and he will pardon your offences." With these words she disappeared, and the heavens were shut, leaving Hermas trembling and horror-stricken.

He remained for some time in a state of great consternation. "If my thoughts of Rhoda are reckoned as sins," he said to himself, "how can I possibly be saved?" While he was thus meditating, there appeared to him a great white chair of white wool on which sat an aged lady clothed in brightly shining raiment and holding in her hand a book.

"Hail, Hermas," she said to him.

"Hail, lady," he replied.

"Why are you so downcast?" she asked. "You who are always so cheerful?"

"Because a gracious lady accused me of sinning against her."

"Certainly something about her came into your heart," replied the aged one, "and such thoughts are evil. But the real reason that God is angry with you is that you have allowed your sons to grow up in wickedness. Turn them from their sinful ways by constantly admonishing them. If they repent they will be saved."

She then offered to read to him from her book, and on his consenting she bade him be attentive. The first part of her reading consisted of terrifying words, such as no man could bear, but the last part was profitable and gentle, and easy to remember. When she had finished she rose, and four young men appeared who carried her chair away to the east. She called Hermas to her, and putting her hand on his breast, asked if her reading had pleased him. Hermas replied that the last part was pleasing but the first part was hard and harsh. She explained that the last part was for the righteous, the first part for heathens and apostates. Immediately two men appeared, lifted her in their arms and carried her away towards the east, where the chair had gone. As she disappeared she called out to him, "Be manful, Hermas."

Next year, at the same season, he was again on the road to Cumae, and again a spirit carried him to the same desert region he had visited before. The same lady again appeared to him, but this time she looked younger. She had her little book in her hand, and was walking to and fro, reading it. She asked Hermas whether he could repeat what she had read from the book to the elect of God.

"Lady," replied Hermas, "I cannot remember it all, but if you will give me the book I will copy it out."

"Take it," she said, "but give it back to me."

He took it away to a retired place in the country and copied it out letter by letter, for like all ancient writings the words were not separated by spaces and Hermas was unable to make out the syllables. When he had finished the copy an invisible hand snatched the book away and it disappeared. After meditating and praying for fifteen days he was enlightened as to the meaning of the book. It was a further injunction to him to reprove his disobedient children, who would thereupon repent and be saved. As to his wife, she was henceforth to be a sister to him.

In his sleep a beautiful young man appeared to him who asked him who he thought the aged lady was.

"The Sibyl," replied Hermas, for he had seen her on the way to Cumae, the home of the Sibyl.

"You are wrong," replied the young man. "She is the Church: and she seemed aged for she was created first of all things."

Hermas had several other visions of the mysterious lady, the last one particularly terrifying.

He was walking along the Campanian road towards his own farm. He left the highway and proceeded along a foot-path, leaving the road ten furlongs away. This part of the country was easily traversed, unlike the desert of his first vision, and he paused awhile to pray. As he was praying he heard a solemn voice saying, "Doubt nothing, Hermas." He was perplexed by this, for he wondered what occasion for doubt there was. But as he pursued his way he saw in front of him a cloud of dust which he supposed was a herd of cattle, but as the cloud increased in size he began to think it concealed some supernatural portent. Presently the sun gleamed out, and he saw that the dust enveloped a huge sea-monster. It was a hundred feet long, and fiery locusts were streaming out of its mouth. Its head appeared to be covered with tiles of four different colours—black, fire and blood colour, gold, and white. This was enough to frighten anyone, but Hermas recalled the words "Doubt nothing" and advanced courageously upon the beast. It was coming on with such a rush that it might have brought havoc to a city, but when Hermas came near, the huge beast crouched meekly on the ground and merely put out its tongue at Hermas as he passed. When he had gone perhaps thirty feet further, the lady of his visions appeared again. This time she was like a virgin coming out of her bride-chamber. She was all in white, with white sandals, she was veiled up to her forehead, a turban was on her head, and though her countenance was youthful her hair was white. She saluted Hermas, and asked him if he had met anything.

"Yes, lady," he replied. "I met a huge beast who might have destroyed whole tribes, but by the power of the Lord and his great mercy I escaped."

"You escaped," said the lady, "because you trusted in the Lord, and he sent his angel Segri[1] to close the monster's mouth. This beast is the type of a great tribulation which is to come. But those who are pure of heart and cast their cares on the Lord, nothing doubting, will be saved." With these words she departed, but Hermas did not see where she had gone, for he heard a loud crashing behind him and made off with all speed, fearing that the beast was approaching.

So ends the first part of our book. In the second the Shepherd at last makes his appearance.

Hermas had prayed and is sitting on his couch[2] when there

---

[1] Segri: He who shuts. Perhaps suggested by Daniel 6: 22—"My God hath sent his angels and hath shut the lions' mouths."

[2] The respect with which *The Shepherd of Hermas* was regarded in the early days of the Church and the curious literal-mindedness of the early Christians is shown by Tertullian, *c.* A.D. 200, who in his homily on prayer assures his flock that in spite of Hermas it is not necessary to sit down after praying.

appears to him a stately youth, dressed as a shepherd in a cloak of white skin, bearing a scrip and a staff. The vision explains that he is the Angel of Repentance. He brings a special message to Hermas who is to write down his precepts that he may keep them at hand and frequently study them. These are the so-called Mandates.

The Mandates bring us to the main theme of the book—the question of Repentance; a question that much perplexed the early Church, and led to more than one schism. Baptism, of course, washed out all sins committed up to that moment, but what of post-baptismal sins? Would they properly be pardoned? Many thought not, especially with reference to the major sins of murder, adultery, and apostasy. This led to the common habit of postponing baptism to the last possible moment—the death-bed. Such a rite was called "clinical baptism" and rather ill-thought of. Constantine the Great received clinical baptism. But as time went on various concessions were made—in the great persecutions Christianity would hardly have survived if all apostates had been excluded from the Church. Some of the righteous, however, remained intransigent as regards post-baptismal sin, and a large group—the Montanists—broke off from the Church on this question. The great Tertullian was among them. Hermas, though writing before the days when Montanism was at its height, held a different view. Even after baptism sins—even the worst sins—would be forgiven after repentance. "Repentance from sins brings life, but not to repent brings death." But there is only one repentance, and it must be a serious one—a man must not "sin off-hand and repent"—though Hermas is not very decided about such backsliders. "If a man sin often and repent it is unprofitable—such a one shall hardly save his soul." It was this teaching that so outraged Tertullian—he speaks of the book as "that apocryphal Shepherd of adulterers."

The instructions of the Shepherd are given to Hermas in twelve mandates and ten similitudes or parables. Most of the mandates are fairly commonplace—believe in one God, observe purity, be long-suffering, and so forth; but two of them are worth attention. The third mandate, *Love truth*, is not remarkable in itself, but the reaction of Hermas is surprising. When he heard it he wept bitterly, for, said he, "I never yet in my life spoke a true word, but I lived always dishonestly with all men and showed my falsehood to all as truth." He declares that never before had he heard that one should speak the truth. The angel admonishes him to reform—whoever keeps himself from the wickedness of falsehood shall live unto God.

It is a pity that the Fathers did not obey this mandate more exactly. Most of them saw no harm in a "pious fraud," and this kind of untruthfulness was freely imputed to the Apostles, to Jesus Christ, and to God the Father. They were fond of literary forgeries—Rufinus thought nothing of altering his author's words in his translation of Origen, Cyril of Jerusalem complains that his letters were tampered with in his own lifetime, reports of synods were freely falsified, so much so that Harnack says the so-called official documents are "a swamp of mendacity. . . . We are helpless . . . in the face of the systematically corrupted tradition".

The tenth mandate is also interesting. "Put away sorrow from thee," says the Shepherd; and he goes on, "Dost thou not perceive that sorrow is worse than all the spirits . . . ?" This *sorrow* is not the same as sadness; it is rather the ecclesiastical sin of *accidie*, so familiar to the monks of the Middle Ages. By derivation it means "not-caring-ness" and stood for a condition of mental depression. Hermas is told that when he saw his first vision his spirit was broken and he was worn out with grief. This depression the O.E.D. says was primarily "the mental prostration of recluses, induced by fasting and other physical causes", among which was the overpowering heat of midday which often overcame the monks of the desert, so much so that it was frequently called "the noonday demon". It was often identified with sloth—thus we find in medieval writings "accidie which I call sloth. . . ." "It is sloth and called accidie"; but this *sloth*, the fourth of the deadly sins, is not mere laziness, but the overpowering dejection which makes any effort or aspiration to God seem impossible. To us it appears to be a physical condition, which should be treated by proper food and a change of air. But the Fathers, like the inhabitants of Erewhon, considered this physical weakness a sin.

We now come to the last part of *The Shepherd*—the ten parables. These are mostly rather arid allegorical similitudes—trees that bear or do not bear fruit and buildings with well-shaped or ill-shaped stones, and righteous or unrighteous men. The most elaborate is the fifth. A certain man made a vineyard which he handed over to a slave, ordering him to stake it. The slave did so, and then, without further orders, dug and weeded it. When the master returned and found that the slave had actually done more than had been required of him he gave him his freedom and made him co-heir with his own son. He also invited him to a banquet, and the slave, having eaten what he required, distributed the rest among his fellow-servants. This parable has two interpretations. The first points out that those who do good works in excess of what is commanded—works of supererogation[1]—win special honour from God. Moreover the true fast is not from food but from evil. That being achieved it is good on certain days to eat only bread and water and give the money that is thus saved to the poor. There is, however, a further interpretation. The owner of the vineyard is God the Father, his son is the Holy Spirit, the virtuous slave is made the Son as a reward for his holy life. But this interpretation is somewhat confused and obscure, and seems to be decidedly heretical.

The scene of the ninth similitude is Arcadia. It is a long and not particularly interesting allegorical account of the building of

[1] The Church of England does not recognise such works. "Voluntary works . . . over and above God's commandments which they call 'works of supererogation' cannot be taught without arrogancy and impiety"—*Thirty-nine Articles*, 14.

the Church, but it contains a very curious episode. The building was assisted by twelve virgins "clothed in linen tunics and suitably girded, having their right shoulders bare, as if they were to carry some burden"—that is, the stones for the building. A great deal of work is carried out and eventually the Shepherd departs commending Hermas to the virgins. When night falls Hermas says he will depart, but the virgins reply,

" 'Thou wast given into our charge, thou mayst not depart from us.'

" 'Where then,' said I, 'shall I remain?'

" 'Thou shalt sleep with us,' say they, 'as a brother not as a husband, for thou art our brother and henceforward we will dwell with thee, for we love thee dearly.'

" But I was ashamed to stay with them. And she that seemed the chief of them began to kiss and embrace me, and the others seeing her embraces began themselves to kiss me and lead me round the tower and sport with me. And I seemed to have grown young again, and began on my part to sport with them. For some of them carolled, some danced and some sang; and I, keeping silence, walked with them in a circle round the tower and was merry with them. And when evening came they would not let me go and I stayed the night with them and slept beside the tower. And the virgins spread their tunics on the ground and made me lie down in the midst of them. . . ."

Honi soit qui mal y pense. For these virgins were, of course, twelve great virtues—Faith, Simplicity, Purity and so forth. To co-habit with such ladies was all to the good.

Nevertheless there is something that seems to us peculiar and somewhat unsavoury in this detailed account of the familiarities between the holy man and the troop of virgins. The story is, in fact, an allusion to a curious custom of the early Church— the associations of virgins—men and women—as a form of asceticism.

The story of Hermas ends by the appearance of an angel in the house of Hermas, accompanied by the Shepherd. The angel addresses a little homily to him, advising him to profit by all that has been shown him. "Whosoever shall walk in these commandments," he says, "shall live, and be happy in his life. . . ." "And when he had finished speaking with me he rose . . . and departed. . . . He said, however, that he would send the shepherd and the virgins back again to my house."

The Epistle of Barnabas

We read of Barnabas in the *Acts of the Apostles* as a companion of Saint Paul, but no one now supposes he was the author of this Epistle. It is an anonymous work, though we can gather something about him from what he says. He was apparently a layman for he repeatedly says, "I am no teacher" —"I am one of yourselves," and he appears to have been an Alexandrian Jew, a convert to Christianity.

Readers of the Acts of the Apostles and of Paul's epistles will be aware of the difficulties that arose in the very first years of Christianity between the Jewish and the Gentile Christians. These difficulties were not soon smoothed out. For at least a hundred years there remained a body of Jewish Christians who refused to give up the Jewish Law and looked with angry suspicion on Paul's teaching of the new Christian liberty. Their opponents felt that the position was a difficult one. Christianity was obviously based on the teaching of the Old Testament, in which the Law was of supreme importance. And yet for Gentiles the manifold regulations of Judaism, beginning with circumcision and continuing into minute and stringent rules of everyday life, would have proved a serious obstacle to conversion. Two books remain as witness to the efforts of the Church in persuading the Jews to give up their devotion to the Law. One of these, the *Epistle to the Hebrews,* eventually found its way into the New Testament. It is the work of a learned man and addressed to men of a theological and philosophical turn of mind, and in spite of its literary merit and lofty rhetoric could hardly be expected to appeal to the ordinary man. The *Epistle of Barnabas*, though written with the same object, is altogether different in outlook. The author—"no teacher"—"one of yourselves"—has a plain, straightforward argument to bring forward, which whether convincing or not would present no metaphysical difficulties to a simple believer. His thesis is that the Law, though valid in itself, was never understood by the Jews. It requires interpretation. His interpretation—which he gives in detail—is allegorical and to us appears fantastic; but it is to be supposed that it appealed to his contemporaries, for it is the method adopted by nearly all the early Fathers in expounding the Old Testament. It would be wearisome to give the whole of his exposition; a few samples will be enough to show the lines of his argument.

He is speaking of the rite of circumcision, and very correctly points out that many others besides Jews had this custom. Syrians, Arabs, Egyptians and other heathens were circumcised—it is by no means a special mark of the Jews. Why then do we hear of it in the old Testament? We are told, "Abraham circumcised ten, eight and three hundred men of his household" (Gen. 17: 23–27). We should interpret it as follows, remembering that numbers were represented in Greek by letters. Ten: I, eight: H (the Greek form of the E in Jesus). Eighteen therefore stands for the Lord. Three hundred: T, which plainly stands for the cross, and the whole prefigures the Crucifixion. A pedantic reasoner might of course argue that God would be unlikely to address Abraham in Greek, but this is not a consideration that would worry Barnabas.

He goes on to discuss the food laws of the Jews. When Moses forbade the people to eat the flesh of pigs he did not mean it literally. No, he meant: "Do not behave like pigs." Other forbidden foods are birds of prey—do not be robbers—lamprey, polypus and cuttlefish which are condemned to live at the bottom of the sea and thus resemble the wickedest of men—the hare, which grows a new anus every year, is like a pederast; the hyena, which changes its sex every year, and the weasel which conceives through the mouth, are also, naturally, to be avoided.

These specimens of how Barnabas expounds the scriptures will no doubt suffice.

Two Early Martyrs—Ignatius and Polycarp

Towards the beginning of the second century a certain Ignatius was the bishop of Antioch. Eusebius[1] says he was the third bishop, St. Peter having been the first. He names himself "Ignatius, called Theophorus", which may mean *God bearer* or *God borne* according to whether it is accented Theo′phorus or Theopho′rus. It seems probable that it should be *God bearer*, an expression he himself uses in his epistle to the Ephesians—"You are all God-bearers." The accent appears to have been misplaced early, as there is a tradition that Ignatius was the child whom Christ presented to the disciples as the model of humility,[2] and hence received the name *God borne*.

About A.D. 110, in the reign of Trajan, a persecution of the Christians broke out in Antioch, and Ignatius was arrested and sent in chains to Rome, to be thrown to the lions. He was guarded on his journey by ten soldiers who treated him harshly—he says they were "ten leopards". His journey was through Philadelphia to Smyrna, where he was allowed a respite, perhaps to recover from his hardships. The bishop of Smyrna at this time was Polycarp, of whom we hear a good deal in Eusebius. The date of his birth presents a curious problem. We are told that at the date of his martyrdom he had been a Christian for eighty-six years. The martyrdom probably took place in 155 and therefore he must have been baptized in 69. It seems highly improbable that he was more than two or

---

[1] The first church historian (*c.* 260–340), who in his Ecclesiastical History has preserved many fragments that would otherwise have been lost.
[2] Mark 9: 36.

three at that date, and we may therefore suppose that he was born between 67 and 69, and that his parents were converts of Saint Paul in one of his missionary journeys in Asia Minor. But this is guess-work. There are also accounts that associate him with St. John. Irenaeus, who, Eusebius tells us, was a pupil of Polycarp's, says he was made bishop by St. John, who is said to have lived at Ephesus.[1] Irenaeus says as a boy he knew Polycarp very well. He remembers the place "where he sat and disputed, how he came in and went out, his character, his outward appearance, the discourses he made to the people, how he reported his intercourse with John, and others who had seen the Lord, how he remembered their words".

The meeting of Ignatius and Polycarp at Smyrna must have been a memorable occasion—Ignatius, writing to Polycarp, says, "I am exceedingly grateful for the privilege I had of seeing your saintly face." Quite possibly Polycarp was his host, and in any case doubtless did all he could to alleviate his sufferings. Many other Christians made their way to Smyrna to visit Ignatius, among them the bishops of Ephesus, Tralles, and Magnesia—altogether we have the names of ten. Before leaving Smyrna Ignatius wrote letters to the Ephesians, the Magnesians and the Trallians, which he no doubt delivered to the bishops to be read to their congregations on their return. These letters are chiefly concerned with warnings against heresy, and injunctions to obey the bishop in everything—for instance, those who wish to marry should obtain his sanction. At Smyrna he also wrote to the Romans. This letter is on a different subject. It is to urge the Christians of Rome not to attempt to save him from martyrdom. He longs to bear witness to his faith. "Suffer me to be the food of wild beasts," he writes. "I am God's wheat, and I am to be ground by

[1]According to various fifth-century writers the apostle John was killed by the Jews at the same time as James. Josephus (A.D. 37–95) dates the death of James in 64. This is one of the arguments for disbelieving the Apostle's authorship of the gospel attributed to him.

the teeth of wild beasts that I may prove Christ's pure bread."[1]

On leaving Smyrna Ignatius was taken north to Troas, on the coast of Asia Minor, and was accompanied by Burrhus, a deacon of Ephesus. At Troas he wrote three more letters— to the Philadelphians, the Smyrneans, and a personal one to Polycarp. He has heard that the persecution at Antioch has ended and he begs the Smyrneans to write to congratulate the Church there. He asks Polycarp to convene a council and select "someone who is dear to you and untiring in his zeal, one qualified for the part of God's courier, and then confer on him the distinction of going to Syria" with the congratulations of the church of Smyrna. He adds that all the churches should do the same, but he himself has not time to write to them to urge this, as he is sailing immediately for Neapolis. These three letters were carried by Burrhus, the deacon.

From Neapolis Ignatius was taken to Philippi, and either there or somewhere on the road he was joined by two other Christians, Zozimus and Rufus, who were probably martyred with him.

Ignatius made a short stay in Philippi, which enabled him and the Christian community there to become acquainted. After this we lose sight of him, but he must have gone on through Macedonia, sailed across to Brundisium, and thence been carried to Rome and his longed-for martyrdom in the Flavian Amphitheatre.

Shortly after Ignatius left Philippi the Philippians wrote to Polycarp. They enclosed—doubtless at the request of Ignatius —a letter of congratulation to Antioch, and requested Polycarp to forward it and to send them copies of any of Ignatius's letters that he had. This Polycarp did, and he requested them to let him have any further news that they might have about Ignatius. That "further news" is unfortunately not extant.

[1] This desire for martyrdom was frequent among the early Christians, and sometimes led to unseemly scenes in which they publicly insulted the official gods, or burst into the law-courts proclaiming their faith and demanding torture and death. Such behaviour had to be forbidden by the Church. *V.* The story of Quintus, p· 32

There does exist an account of the martyrdom of Ignatius, but it is late and unhistorical.

About twenty years later, towards A.D. 135, the Philippians wrote again to Polycarp, telling him of the joy they had experienced at welcoming Ignatius and his fellow prisoners, and giving an account of the conditions in their community. Polycarp in his reply assures them that he shares their joy, and continues his epistle in a vein of exhortation. He chiefly insists on the necessity of keeping the faith pure and avoiding avarice and a love of money. He is led to this by a report that a former presbyter of theirs, Valens, and his wife had been guilty of some dishonest practices. It would be interesting to know exactly what they did, but no more is told.

The next we hear of Polycarp is concerned with his visit to Rome, about 154, when he must have already been an old man. On this visit he had a discussion with the Pope Anicetus as to the date on which the Crucifixion and Easter should be observed. It was the custom in the East to celebrate Good Friday on the 14th of Nizam, and they were hence called *Quartodecimans*. The trouble was that the 14th of Nizam might fall on any day of the week; in the West it was held that the Crucifixion must be celebrated on a Friday and Easter Day on a Sunday. Neither of the two disputants convinced the other, but they remained on friendly terms and took Communion together; Anicetus made no objection to Polycarp's celebrating the Holy Days in Rome on his chosen dates. As Eusebius tell us, "They parted from each other in peace, for the peace of the whole church was kept by those who observed and those who did not." Unfortunately this spirit of tolerance was not maintained and the Quartodecimans were eventually excommunicated. It was during his stay in Rome that he encountered the heretic Marcion, against whose teachings he had warned the Philippians. Marcion, meeting Polycarp in the street, said to him, "Do you recognise me?" To which he replied, "I do. I recognise the first-born of Satan."

The following year—155—is the year of Polycarp's martyrdom. Of this we have a very full acount. It is in the form of
an epistle to the Philomelians who had asked for the details
of Polycarp's death. It appears to have been composed by
an eyewitness, Marcianus, and is surprisingly free from
exaggerated miracles.

At this time, in the reign of Antoninus Pius, a persecution of
the Christians started in the neighbourhood of Smyrna. Polycarp, urged by his congregation, withdrew from the city and
concealed himself in a neighbouring farm belonging to friends.
One day, while he was at prayer, he had a vision in which he
saw his pillow in flames; turning to his companions he said
calmly, "I see that I must be burnt at the stake." The chief of
police, who by a curious coincidence was called Herod, went
in search of him, accompanied by a band of armed soldiers "as
against a thief" (Matt. 26: 55). They seized and tortured one
of his slaves, who told them where his master was hidden, and
towards evening they found him, concealed in a small room
under the roof of the house. Many of the soldiers were em-
barrassed at finding they had to arrest such an old man:
and somewhat reluctantly seated him on an ass and escorted
him to the city. There he was met by Herod and his father
Nicetas, who transferred him to their carriage and drove towards the arena. On the way they reasoned with him, trying
to persuade him to save himself by offering incense to the Lord
Caesar. "There can really be no harm in it," they urged, "and
you will escape dreadful penalties." At first Polycarp made no
answer, but finally replied, "I shall not do what you advise."
Herod and Nicetas became annoyed, and pushed him out of the
carriage so roughly that he bruised his shin. He gave no sign
that he felt the injury, but walked briskly towards the arena.

Meanwhile the games had been started and were in full
swing. One of the Christians, a Phrygian called Quintus, had
pushed himself before the proconsul, Quadratus, denouncing
himself, and urging others to come forward of their own

accord. But when he saw the wild beasts he lost heart and gave way to the entreaties of the proconsul. He took the oath in Caesar's name and offered incense, thus showing the rashness and conceit of those who voluntarily accuse themselves. Far other was the behaviour of the lad Germanicus. When he was actually in the arena, wrestling with a wild animal, Quadratus urged him to have pity on his own youth; but Germanicus forcibly dragged the beast towards himself, desiring to escape as soon as possible from a world full of depravity. But the crowd was enraged by the spectacle and called out: "Away with the atheists who do not worship our gods! Bring out Polycarp!"

At this moment Polycarp entered the arena, and as he did so a voice was heard saying: "Be strong, Polycarp, play the man." Nobody saw the speaker but the Christians who heard it said it was a voice from heaven. When Polycarp was led up to the tribunal, Quadratus tried the usual persuasions. "Say 'Away with the atheists!'" he began. Polycarp looked grimly at the howling mob of bloodthirsty spectators, waved his hand towards them and said sternly: "Away with the atheists!" The proconsul persisted. "Take the oath and revile Christ and I will set you free." "For eighty-six years I have served Him," replied Polycarp. "How dare I now revile my King!" After some further argument the proconsul gave up his attempts, and ordered his herald to announce from the centre of the arena: "Polycarp has confessed that he is a Christian." At this the fury of the mob became frenzied, and they shouted to Philip, the master of the games: "Let loose a lion on him!" This, however, Philip refused to do, for he said he had already closed the hunting sports. "Then let him be burnt," shouted the crowd, and Polycarp remembered his burning pillow.

The proconsul gave orders for him to be burnt and the onlookers rushed to get firewood from shops and bath houses. The pyre was soon prepared, Polycarp was fastened in the centre of it and after he had uttered a short prayer and thanksgiving the fire was lit. A great flame shot up; but in marvellous fashion it did not burn the martyr, but bellied out like a ship's sail in a breeze, surrounding his body as with a wall. Seeing that he could not be burnt an executioner was ordered to stab him. Immediately a stream of blood gushed out and extinguished the flames and at the same moment a dove issued from him and flew up to heaven. This appearance of a dove is the only undoubted miracle in the account. It may be a later addition, for Eusebius, who quotes the epistle verbatim, does not mention it. At the very moment when Polycarp expired, Irenaeus, who was in Rome at the time, heard a heavenly voice announce: "Polycarp is dead."

"Such," says the epistle, "is the story of the blessed Polycarp, who suffered martyrdom at Smyrna, with eleven others from Philadelphia."

Papias

Our next writer is a mysterious figure, of whom we know with certainty but little. His writings are extant only as fragmentary quotations and the true meaning of what he wrote is obscure, as the quotations are presented to us apart from their context. The very title of his book is by no means clear: *Exposition of the Logia of the Lord. Five books.* Have we here a subjective or objective genitive? Is the exposition concerned with what the Lord said, or with what was said about him? We have no way of deciding. The scantiness and obscurity of our data is the more unfortunate as Papias was in a position to provide us with peculiarly interesting information as to the earliest traditions of Christianity. He was probably born about A.D. 60 and composed his book about A.D. 100. He was thus, roughly speaking, a contemporary of Ignatius and Polycarp. He was the bishop of Hierapolis, a town of Asia Minor, situated at the junction of two important roads crossing each other from East to West and from South-East to North-West. He was thus in the best locality for collecting the traditions of early Christian missionaries who streamed out of Palestine into Asia Minor, following in the footsteps of St. Paul. He himself tells us that he obtained his information by questioning the "presbyters" who had known the Lord, or their closest associates. "I took for granted," he says, "that book knowledge would not help me so much as a living voice." Alas, when the voice is no longer living we have to depend on what is written; and in the case of Papias the written word too has to a great extent vanished.

It is from Papias that we learn that "the presbyter John said: When Mark became Peter's interpreter he wrote down, though not in order (οὐ μέντοι τάξει), all that he remembered of what the Lord had said or done". And further that "Matthew compiled the Logia in Hebrew and each one translated it as best he could". These important descriptions of the origins of the first two Gospels have led to endless disputes. Who was "the presbyter John"? In giving the account of Mark's gospel was he—as Loisy thinks—trying to bring discredit on Mark and Peter? What is the correct meaning of μέντοι τάξει? Is it *in order* or *verbatim*? What is meant by the *logia* Matthew is said to have compiled? Does Papias mean they were *translated* by a variety of teachers, or *expounded*—explained? If we had the whole of Papias's book these mysteries would perhaps be cleared up. But Eusebius, from whom most of the quotations come, had the lowest opinion of Papias, whom he considered "a man of very meagre intelligence". This was probably because Papias held views, later condemned by the Church, on the Last Days. Eusebius himself does not tell us what these views were, but Irenaeus—about fifty years later than Papias—quotes him as follows:

"Concerning the last days the Lord announced: A time is coming when vineyards will spring up, each having ten thousand branches, and on each branch ten thousand shoots, and on each shoot ten thousand clusters, and in each cluster ten thousand grapes, and every grape when pressed will yield two hundred and fifty gallons of wine. And when any one of the Saints shall take hold of one of the clusters another cluster will cry out: 'I am a better cluster—take me, to bless the Lord.' In the same way (the Lord declared) a seed of wheat will produce ten thousand ears, and each ear will have ten thousand grains, and each grain will produce ten pounds of clear, pure flour. And all other fruit-trees and seeds and grass will produce in similar proportions, and all animals which feed on these products of the earth will become peaceable and friendly to each other and be completely subject to man."

"Papias adds," says Irenaeus, "these things can be believed by believers. And when Judas, the traitor, would not believe, and asked, 'How can the Lord bring about such growths?' the Lord replied, 'Those who live to that time shall see.' "

Papias seems to have taken a special interest in Judas Iscariot, concerning whom many legends were current. The New Testament has two different accounts of his death. In Matthew's Gospel we are told that he repented of his treachery and having returned the thirty pieces of silver to the priests went out and hanged himself. The priests however refused to put the money into the treasury because it was the price of blood, but they spent it in buying a potter's field, to bury strangers in. And because it had been bought with blood money it was called "the field of blood" (Matt. 27: 3–10).

Acts has a different story. Judas never repented. He kept the money and himself bought the potter's field with it and there "falling headlong he burst asunder in the midst, and all his bowels gushed out". This was the reason that the place was called Aceldama, the field of blood (Acts 1: 18, 19).

Papias relates the end of Judas, and his story is obviously based on Acts rather than on Matthew, though he makes a half-hearted attempt at harmonising the two. Judas, it would appear, only attempted to hang himself; he was cut down before death supervened. He lived on, but he developed a loathsome disease. "His body bloated to such an extent that even where a wagon passes with ease he was not able to pass—no, not even his bloated head could get through. His eyelids . . . swelled to such a size that he could not see the light at all, nor could his eyes be detected even by a physician's optical instrument." Further repulsive details follow. "Finally, after suffering an agony of pain and punishment he went, as they say, to *his own place*, and owing to the stench the place has been deserted and uninhabited till now. . . ."

We may mention that Irenaeus knew of a heretical sect called Cainites, who for some incomprehensible reasons of their own, looked upon Judas as a quasi-divine being, and studied a work which they called The Gospel of Judas.

II

Apologies

THE writers we have studied so far addressed themselves to their brethren—they produced Christian writings for Christian readers. We now come to a group of authors who were engaged in defending their religion and attacking paganism or Judaism—the Apologists. Their work became necessary owing to a development in the anti-Christian policy of the government.

The celebrated persecution of the Christians under Nero in A.D. 64 was carried out by accusing them of arson. This was the specific crime with which they were charged, and for which they were executed in such numbers and with such cruelty that, Tacitus (*fl.c.* 55–120) tells us, the Roman people were finally disgusted and began to feel sympathy for the sufferers. The next persecution on an important scale was that of Domitian. Dio Cassius tells us that in A.D. 95 the consul Clemens and his wife Domitilla were tried and condemned on a charge of sacrilege, and a great many others were put to death or deprived of their property for the same offence. All modern writers are agreed that Clemens and Domitilla were Christians; they were given formal trials because they were Roman citizens. It appears certain that many others of inferior rank suffered under Domitian, probably without trial and by administrative action. The matter is however somewhat obscure, and it is only when we reach the reign of Trajan that a flood of light is thrown on the official attitude towards Christianity. In A.D. 112 Pliny became governor of the province of Bithynia-Pontus. Bithynia had to a large extent adopted Christianity, so much so that the temples were almost deserted and the sale of fodder for the sacrificial beasts had come to a stand-still. The Christians were denounced to the authorities and those who admitted their faith were executed. Those who denied the charge, or recanted and cursed Christ, put Pliny in a difficulty. He ascertained that they had not been guilty of specific crimes, kept them under arrest, and wrote to ask Trajan how he should proceed. The Emperor replied that Pliny had been right in executing those who persisted in declaring themselves Christians; those who repented were not to be punished; the Christians were not to be sought out, or proceeded against if their accusers were anonymous.

This correspondence shows us much that is interesting. The feeling against the Christians among the heathen population was often because their teaching interfered with trade. In Bithynia they were doubtless denounced by the traders in cattle fodder. In the same way the silversmiths of Ephesus had caused a riot against St. Paul because his preaching was opposed to the idol worship of Diana. The Christians, whose rites were secret and included a Communion in which they said they consumed the body and blood of Christ, were believed to be cannibals, to kill small children for their rites, and to commit incest in the darkness of their ceremonial. It was only by persistent enquiry that Pliny became convinced of their innocence of these crimes; the same accusation was preferred against them, all through the second and third centuries.[1] From Trajan's letter we see that they were not officially charged with any definite crime—they were punished for the Name, which was taken to imply sacrilege and treason. If they continued to declare that they were Christians no further enquiries were necessary. They were self-condemned, and their punishment followed automatically. This attitude of the Roman state was inherited by the Church when in its turn it obtained supreme power.[2]

It was against this attitude that most of the early apologists appealed, in books presented to the Emperors. Many of these

---

[1] A Vanished Sect—The Montanists, p. 172.

[2] "The repression of heresy by the State, so long universally acknowledged as a necessity, grew out of the same principles as the persecution of Early Christianity by the Roman Empire." Duchesne, vol. I, p. 82 n. The same principle—punishment for the name—seems to underlie some proceedings in America against the Communists.

works have disappeared, others are of no great interest—we shall mention here Justin Martyr, Tatian, Theophilus of Antioch who wrote during the reigns of Antoninus Pius, 138–161, and Marcus Aurelius, 161–180, and Minucius Felix, whose date is uncertain and has been placed by different authorities in 180 or 240.

Justin Martyr

Justin, who lived towards the middle of the second century, began life as a philosopher. He studied the teachings of Pythagoras, the Stoics, the Peripatetics and the Platonists, and finally, it having been pointed out to him that the Jewish prophecies of the Old Testament were fulfilled in Christ, he became a Christian. One of his books, *Trypho*, is an attempt to convert the Jews by the same reasoning. His two Apologies, addressed to Antoninus Pius, urge the Emperor to abandon the practice of punishing Christians for the Name. They are not, he says, guilty of cannibalism and incest, but if it is proved that they commit crimes let them be punished like other criminals, not merely for being Christians. Justin is the first of the Fathers to have noticed the resemblances between Greek myths and Christianity. He has an ingenious way of accounting for this. The demons studied the Old Testament scriptures, and realising that they would later be verified in the life of Christ, themselves produced myths to imitate the truth. They said that Bacchus was the son of the chief god, Jupiter, that he was torn to pieces and ascended into heaven. They told of Perseus who was born of a virgin, and Aesculapius who cured many men of their diseases and raised them from the dead. In the same way the demons instigated the heathen to perform a pseudo-baptismal rite, by washing and sprinkling themselves before entering their temples. The worshippers of Mithras, led on by devils, imitate the holy Eucharist by partaking of bread and wine in their initiation rites.

The demons still deceive men, by stirring up false teachers

and persuading men to worship them. They put forward a Samaritan Simon Magus[1] who by their help performed many magical deeds and was worshipped by the Romans as a god. There was, says Justin, a statue erected in his honour, on the Tiber, between the two bridges, bearing this inscription:

SIMONI

DEO SANCTO

(To Simon, the Holy God)

The interesting thing about this report of Justin's is that in 1574 the pedestal of a statue was found at Rome, on the island of San Sebastian, on which were the words:

SEMONI

SANCO

DEO FIDIO

SANCUS

This is interpreted by modern antiquarians as a dedication to the Sabine god, Semo Sancus. Justin's mistake is easily understood.

Justin makes an allusion to another Roman monument, still in existence—the Column of Antonine. He quotes a spurious edict of Marcus Aurelius, forbidding the persecution of the Christians, on account of a miracle performed by them during the Marcomannian war. The actual event is well attested, and is fully described by Dio Cassius. The Marcomannian war was a conflict between the Roman Empire and a confederation of Germanic and Sarmatian tribes who invaded north Italy towards 167. This war, a serious menace to the Empire, was still raging at the time of the death of Marcus Aurelius in 180. The episode which gave rise to the story of the Christian miracle took place when a Roman army was surrounded by

---

[1] *V. Clement and the Clementines*, p. 78; Simon Magus at Rome, p. 99.

the Barbarians in a mountainous defile. There had been a long drought and the Romans, entirely deprived of water, were in danger of dying of thirst. Prayers were offered up for their relief, and these prayers were effective. Rain fell in torrents and was caught by the Roman soldiers on their shields and drunk with avidity. The rain, accompanied by a violent thunderstorm, beat in the faces of the enemy, whose ranks were struck by lightning and thrown into disorder. The Romans immediately attacked and won a resounding victory. According to the spurious edict of Marcus Aurelius quoted by Justin, the prayer was offered to the Christian God—"a god of whom I am ignorant" says the spurious Marcus Aurelius. This became a favourite legend among the Christians, many of whom[1] repeat the story, attributing the prayer to the 12th legion, which they say consisted almost entirely of Christians, and which received in consequence the name of *Legio Fulminatrix*—the Thundering Legion. Unfortunately the legion had in reality received this name in the time of Augustus, or at latest in that of Nero. Dio Cassius attributes the successful prayer to an Egyptian priest appealing to Hermes. The base of the Antonine column, constructed towards 175, shows the saving diety to have been Jupiter Pluvius, who may still be seen with torrential rain pouring down from his hair, his beard and his arms.

Tatian

Tatian was a pupil of Justin Martyr, who after Justin's death broke with the Church and founded the heretical sect of the Encratites. His heresy consisted in exaggerated asceticism— marriage was forbidden—and in denying that Adam was saved. In his orthodox days he wrote a defence of Christianity called *Address to the Greeks* (c. 155) in which, like Justin, he attacks the heathen mythology, but with more venom and more wit. It is absurd of the Greeks, he says, to despise the Barbarians, for as a

---

[1] Tertullian Apol. 5; Eusebius 5: 5; Greg. Nyss. Or 11.

matter of fact most of their ideas are derived from them. They learnt astronomy from the Babylonians, magic from the Persians, geometry from the Egyptians, and alphabetic writing from the Phoenicians. Nor did they originate the arts. Orpheus the Thracian was the first poet, the Etruscans the first artists, the Egyptians the first historians, Marsyas and Olympus, two Phrygian peasants, the first flute-players. They are not even agreed as to how to pronounce their own language. The Dorians, the Aeolians, the Ionians and the men of Attica all speak differently—which of all these dialects is really Greek? They use rhetoric to serve injustice and slander, poetry to glorify war and the amours of the gods. Their philosophers were a shady lot. Plato was sold as a slave by Dionysius for his gormandising propensities. Diogenes, who made such a parade of his independence with his tub, was seized by a bowel complaint through eating a raw polypus, and so lost his life by gluttony. To this day the Greek philosophers are inconsistent and contemptible. They leave uncovered one of their shoulders, they let their hair grow long, they cultivate their beards, their nails are like the claws of wild beasts. Some of them receive 600 gold pieces a year from the Emperor, not for rendering any useful service, but so that they should not grow their beards without being paid for it.

Tatian goes on to jeer at the Greeks for their belief in astrology which teaches that men's fate and behaviour is controlled by the stars. These stars are many of them said to be metamorphosed animals—the Dog of Erigone, the Scorpion of Artemis, Callisto when she had been turned into a Bear. Were the heavens dark before these metamorphoses had taken place?

The amusements of the heathen are as vile as their beliefs. "I have seen a man," he says, describing the theatrical displays, "giving himself all the airs of an affected woman—rolling his eyes, gesticulating wildly, raving with his face covered with mud: sometimes impersonating Aphrodite, sometimes Apollo ... an actor of murders, a chronicler of adultery, a storehouse of madness . . . and yet such a man is praised by all." Displays of boxing are also to be condemned in which men give each other blows for no reason whatever. Worse still are the gladiator shows. One man collects a legion of bloodstained murderers, and these ruffians are watched and admired by large crowds; and if anyone misses one of these murderous exhibitions he grieves because he was not a spectator of wicked, impious and abominable deeds.

In fact the heathen are admirers of all sorts of wickedness and folly. They have raised statues to the tyrant Bhalaris who devoured sucklings, to the fratricides Polynices and Eteocles, to Ganymede the hermaphrodite. The women they honour by statues are even more degraded. "Why should I contemplate with admiration the figure of a woman who bore thirty children . . . whom the Romans compared to a sow and who was, they say, thought worthy of a mystic worship? . . . What a noble infant did Glaucippe present to you, who brought forth a prodigy as is shown by her statue . . . but if she did give birth to an elephant is that a reason why she should receive public honours?"

With these immoralities and follies Tatian compares the beliefs of the Christians. They worship one God, a pure and ineffable spirit. He who is in want of nothing is not to be offered gifts and bloody sacrifices. Their religion is more ancient than that of the Greeks, for Moses lived before Homer. The Christians lead purer lives than the heathen. They have renounced worldly things and obey the commands of God. "Not only do the rich among us study philosophy but the poor are taught freely. We admit all who desire to hear, even old women and youths; persons of every age are treated by us with respect, and every kind of licentiousness is avoided. And in speaking we utter no falsehoods. . . . Laugh if you please; but you will have to weep hereafter."

Theophilus of Antioch

Theophilus was a contemporary of Tatian; according to Eusebius he was the bishop of Antioch in about 160. His Apology is contained in three letters, addressed to his friend Autolycus. It is a curious fact that he never mentions the name of Christ, though he discusses at some length the word *Christian*. It will be remembered that according to Acts the followers of the Lord were first called Christians at Antioch—probably as a derisive epithet—and we may note that the first appearance of the name in Patristic writings is in one of the letters of Ignatius, also a bishop of Antioch.

The word *Christ* seems to have caused difficulties in the Greek mind. It means "the Anointed", and is a translation of the Aramaic *meshiakh*, transliterated *messiah*. In Old Testament times the King and the High Priest were anointed, and *the Anointed One* became an ordinary expression meaning the King. This usage is still retained in English, as we may see from the fact that the Vicar of Bray taught his flock that

> Kings were by God appointed,
> And damned are they that do resist
> Or touch the Lord's anointed.

In later times the Jews came to console themselves for their misfortunes and sufferings by the belief that an ideal King—perhaps a quasi-divine being—would come to rule over them, and to this visionary king they gave the name of Messiah. The word Messiah, and its Greek translation, Christ, both appear throughout the New Testament. In the gospels it is usually preceded by the article—*the* Christ—and is used as a title. This title would, of course, be readily understood by the Jews, but the Gentiles, who had no custom of ceremonial anointing, would be puzzled by the usage. Consequently Saint Paul, in addressing the Gentile world, uses the expression

Jesus Christ and the word Christ, as with us, was considered a surname. This happened the more easily, as χριστός—a strange word to the Greeks—resembled the familiar word χρηστός (good, useful), a common name for a slave. Suetonius, *c*. 120, states that Claudius expelled the Jews from Rome because "they were constantly causing disturbances at the instigation of Chrestus". Nobody knows whether this means a real Jewish agitator, or alludes to disputes between the Jews and the Christians. St. Paul in his epistle to Philemon says of the slave Onesimus (profitable) he was in the past unprofitable—ἄχρηστος—but is now profitable—εὔχρηστος—he has become a Christian. Theophilus, too, plays on the word. "You call me a Christian," he says, "as if it were a damnable name to bear; but I for my part declare that I am indeed a Christian, hoping to be serviceable—εὔχρηστος—to God." He goes on to point out that what is anointed—χριστός—is also useful—χρηστός—and gives as examples ships which must be caulked, the gymnast who must be rubbed with oil, all ornaments, that must be anointed and burnished. This elaborate defence of the word is interesting, as showing that as late as the middle of the second century the word Christian had still somewhat ridiculous associations.

We may also note that Theophilus is the first of the Fathers to use the word Trinity in reference to the Godhead. He does not, however, explain it according to the later usage of Father, Son, and Holy Ghost, but speaks of "the Trinity of God, His word and His wisdom".

Like the other Apologists Theophilus condemns the heathen mythology for its immortality and absurdity. He denounces the Egyptians for worshipping reptiles, cattle, wild beasts, birds and river fishes; and even foot-baths and disgraceful noises. (Perhaps an allusion to Echo, who was punished for her improper loquacity.) Some heathens even worship Satan, who led Eve into sin. This is shown by their shouting "Eva" at their Bacchanalian orgies.

Theophilus is further notable as the first of the Christian chronologists. He made elaborate calculations based on the data in the Old Testament, and arrived at the conclusion that the world was created in the year 5529 B.C. Archbishop Usher, who made similar calculations, arrived at the date 4004 B.C. for the creation. Both Theophilus and the Archbishop, however, admit that their results may not be exactly correct, as "the odd months and days are not set down in the sacred books". This doubtless accounts for the discrepancy between them.

Minucius Felix

Our next apologist is an unusually interesting figure. His date is uncertain and is much disputed—it is doubtfully placed between A.D. 160 and 200. In any case he was one of the first Christians, if not the very first, to write in Latin. We know but little of him. *The Octavius* is his only extant work, though Jerome speaks of another, *De Fato*, doubtfully attributed to him and in any case now lost. He was a Roman lawyer, a convert to Christianity, and is generally believed to have been an African by birth. *The Octavius* is a short dialogue, modelled on Cicero's *De Natura Deorum*, and recounts a conversation between three friends, Minucius, Octavius and Caecilius, in the course of which Caecilius is converted to Christianity. The line of argument pursued by Octavius has proved a stumbling block to many modern theologians. There is no mention of Christ or the Crucifixion, no reference to any specifically Christian doctrine except the Resurrection, no exposition of the Christian mysteries. Octavius supports his case by quoting from the classical poets and philosophers rather than from the Hebrew prophets. Many explanations have been offered for the unique character of this Apology, into which we will not enter in detail. It may, however, be noted that at the end of the dialogue, Caecilius, who declares himself converted to Christianity by the arguments of Octavius, adds, "There are still certain details which must be discussed to make my instruction complete." *The Octavius* is best thought of, not as a finished defence of Christianity, but as an introduction to the Christian philosophy and a plea addressed to the educated Roman to reconsider the matter in a sympathetic spirit.

For our purpose the most charming part of the dialogue lies in the opening chapters. Minucius tells us that his friend Octavius is dead. He describes in touching terms their mutual affection and sympathy, and how now that they are parted by death he dwells fondly on their past intercourse. In particular he loves to recall the conversation in which Octavius turned their friend Caecilius from heathendom to the true faith.

"Octavius had come to Rome on business, and also to see me. He had left his home, his wife and his children—his children, still in the age of innocence, when their broken speech is so charming, all the sweeter for the havoc they make of the language with their faltering tongues. Words cannot express the joy with which I greeted the unexpected arrival of my dearest friend."

After one or two days in Rome, they took advantage of the legal vacation to make an excursion to Ostia, a favourite summer resort and bathing place of well-to-do Romans. They took with them a common friend, Caecilius, and set out one morning at dawn to walk towards the sea. "The soft breeze was invigorating, and the feeling of our gentle footsteps sinking into the yielding sand was peculiarly delightful. All at once Caecilius caught sight of an image of Serapis, and following the common superstition put his hand to his mouth and kissed it." Serapis was an Egyptian god, very popular in Rome at that time. The usual way of saluting and paying homage to a god was to kiss the hand, and when Octavius saw the action of Caecilius he turned to Minucius and rebuked him for not having taught his friend the folly of worshipping idols.

"While Octavius was speaking we continued our walk and reached a point half-way between the town and the sea, where the open beach, washed by the gentle waves, seemed to be laid out as a promenade. The sea is always restless even when the winds are still, and though it did not reach the land in white, foaming waves it advanced curling and swelling. We were delighted to feel it rippling round our feet when we stepped into the water's edge—the waves alternately advancing sportively towards our feet and then flowing back, re-absorbed in the sea. We strolled quietly along the gently curving beach, beguiling the way with Octavius's tales of his voyage. After we had gone some distance, we turned and retraced our steps until we reached a spot where some boats had been hauled up and placed on wooden supports, out of the mud. There we saw some boys enjoying a game of ducks and drakes." Minucius gives a detailed description of the game, which the boys were playing with shells. The friends watched the game with some amusement; Caecilius alone took no interest in it, but stood by absorbed in thought, serious and gloomy. Minucius asked him what was the matter. He replied that he had been much hurt by what Octavius had said about his saluting Serapis. He proposed that they should thrash the matter out thoroughly, in a serious but amicable fashion. "Let us sit down," he continued, "on that rocky mole sticking out into the sea, which has been made as a breakwater for the bathing place. We can rest there after our walk and discuss the matter thoroughly." Octavius and Minucius agreed; the three friends sat down and the discussion proceeded.

Caecilius begins his attack on Christianity by declaring that the Christians are ignorant and uneducated. They worship an ass's head, a cross and a criminal who was executed for his crimes. He goes on with old calumnies of secret vices concealed in the darkness of their mysteries. Their God, who they say is omnipotent, is unable to protect them from the Romans.

The problems they pretend to solve are in reality insoluble, for they transcend the limits of human understanding.

Octavius in reply points out that much Christian teaching is accepted by heathen philosophers. The unity of God, His eternity and omniscience are recognised by many of them. The greatness of Rome, supposed to be owing to her gods, was built up by robbery and the violation of justice and religion. The gods are in fact wicked demons. The Christians do not commit crimes—their lives are pure and unstained; and they accept their earthly sufferings as a test of virtue and a preparation for the life to come.

When Octavius had finished speaking his two friends gazed at him in admiration. Minucius was overwhelmed by his skill in argument, the way in which he quoted from authorities and repelled the attacks of his enemies. As he was turning these things over in his mind, Caecilius burst out.

"Though Octavius is victorious," he cried, "I, too, claim a victory—a victory over error, for I accept your teaching and your sect shall henceforth be mine. . . . But as the sun is already setting we will deal with any further points tomorrow; they will not detain us long since we are agreed on essentials."

The three friends then went home, joyful and contented, Caecilius because he believed, Octavius because he was victorious, Minucius Felix because of the conversion of the one and the victory of the other.

53

III

Apocryphal Writings

During the earlier centuries of the Church a vast number of spurious Gospels, Acts, Epistles and Revelations were produced. These works purported to be written by different apostles and to supplement the teaching of the New Testament. Some were orthodox, some heretical; some contained doctrinal teaching, some were anecdotal in character. For the most part they made their appeal to the ordinary, unlearned Christian of the day, and represented his light reading matter—novels, thrillers, adventure stories. They are full of romance, miracle and magic, and retained their popularity throughout the Middle Ages. They provide in fact the origin of many legends and the subject matter of many religious pictures.

It must be confessed that they do not, strictly speaking, fall within our subject. They are not patristic writings and the Fathers often condemn them, though from time to time they quote them in a more or less approving fashion. They are interesting to us as revealing the popular appeal of Christianity to the ordinary uneducated man, as opposed to the more esoteric speculations of the scholars and theologians.

Gospels of the Infancy

Two second-century books deal with stories of the childhood of the Virgin and the infancy of Christ. They are *The Protevangelium,* and the *Gospel of Thomas.*

* * * *

Joachim and Anna were a rich and virtuous married pair among the Jews. They were strict in their observance of the law, but they were plunged in grief, for they had no children.

At last, in her sorrow, Anna made a vow that if she had a child she would dedicate it to God. Thereupon an angel of the Lord appeared to her and announced that she should conceive and bring forth, and that her seed should be spoken of in the whole world. In due course a child was born; it was a girl, and her parents named her Mary and resolved in accordance with Anna's vow to devote her to the service of God. Accordingly when she was three years old they took her to Jerusalem and presented her to the High Priest, Zachariah. He kissed her and blessed her, and made her sit down on the third step of the altar. And the Lord put grace upon her, and she danced with her feet, and during all the years that she dwelt in the Temple she received food from the hand of an angel.

When Mary was twelve years old and the priests were wondering what to do with her, an angel appeared to Zachariah in the temple. The angel ordered him to assemble all the widowers of Israel, each one bringing with him a rod, and the Lord would give him a sign to show whose wife she should be. Zachariah carried out these instructions, and among the widowers came Joseph, a carpenter, an old man, the father of sons. All the rods were placed on the altar and the High Priest prayed over them. When they were returned to their owners a dove flew out of Joseph's rod and perched upon his head. (In some versions we are told that Joseph's rod burst into flower.) At this sign Zachariah saw that Joseph was the predestined bridegroom of Mary, and handed her over to him. She went to live in his house, but he did not touch her, and leaving her alone he went off to occupy himself with some buildings he was putting up.

About this time the priests decided that a new veil for the temple should be made. It was to be woven of gold and white, linen and silk, scarlet and purple. Seven virgins, amongst whom was Mary, were assembled to do the weaving, and lots were cast as to who should weave the different colours. The scarlet and purple fell to the lot of Mary, and she carried them back to her house.

The story then follows the gospel narrative. We are told of the Annunciation, the Visitation to Elizabeth, Mary's kinswoman and the wife of Zachariah, Joseph's distress at discovering Mary's condition and his dream in which an angel appeared to reassure him.

An episode peculiar to the *Protevangelium* is here inserted. The priests discover that Mary is with child, and Zachariah declares that Joseph and Mary have both sinned, for she had been devoted to the Lord as a virgin. He therefore gives them each a poisoned draught which however has no ill effect. Everyone is amazed, and Zachariah, rightly concluding that they cannot after all have sinned, lets them depart in peace.

We then return to the story of the Nativity, which is very different from the Gospel account. Augustus the King sent forth a decree that all that were in Bethlehem should be recorded. Joseph felt himself in a dilemma as to how he was to record Mary—he was ashamed to call her his wife, and everyone knew she was not his daughter. However he decided to leave the outcome to the Lord. He placed Mary on a she-ass, led by one of his sons, and he himself followed. As they went along Joseph perceived that Mary was sometimes sad and at other times laughing. Astonished, he asked her the cause of this, to which she replied, "It is because I behold two peoples, the one weeping and lamenting and the other rejoicing and exulting."

When they approached Bethlehem Mary asked Joseph to take her down from the ass, for her hour was approaching. The place where they were was desert, but Joseph found a cave into which he put her, and leaving his son in charge went off to find a midwife.

As he walked along a strange marvel befell. He found he could not advance. Looking up he saw that the heavenly bodies were motionless and so too were the birds in the air. A party of workmen were sitting round a dish, some in the act of lifting the food to their mouths, but not lifting it, some chewing the food, but not chewing it, and all gazing up at the sky. A flock of sheep, that were being driven along the road, remained still; the shepherd stood with his staff raised and did not bring it down. A group of kids stood in a stream, their mouths open in the water, and they did not drink. Then suddenly the strange paralysis ended, and all things continued to move as before.

At this moment Joseph saw a woman coming towards him. She was a midwife, and Joseph asked her to come to the cave and attend to Mary. In answer to the midwife's questions he told her that Mary was not his wife—she had conceived by the Holy Ghost. In great astonishment the woman went with Joseph to the cave over which a bright cloud was hanging. Presently the cloud dispersed and a bright light was seen inside the cave. Little by little the light too vanished and a Child appeared taking the breast of his mother. The midwife immediately recognised that these marvels portended the birth of salvation to Israel. As she left the cave she met another woman, Salome, and told her that she had seen a virgin giving birth to a child. Salome however was sceptical, and refused to believe until she had investigated the matter for herself. When she approached the Child she cried out in horror that her hand was being consumed by fire. She realised the sinful nature of her incredulity, and falling on her knees prayed to God to forgive her. Immediately an angel appeared, saying, "Salome, the Lord has heard thee. Stretch forward thy hand towards the Child, and thou shalt be cured." Salome approached and took him up, crying out, "I will worship him, for he is a great king born to Israel." Immediately as she lifted him up her hand was healed; for her sin was forgiven.

This story of the presence of a midwife at the Nativity was current in the second century as we know from Clement of Alexandria who says, "After she [Mary] had brought forth, some say that she was attended by a midwife, and was found to be a virgin." There was however a contrary tradition. Mary was delivered painlessly, by God himself, without the help of a midwife. In the Odes of Solomon, probably written in the second century, we read:

> And the Virgin became a mother with great mercy;
> And she travailled and brought forth a Son without
> incurring pain:
> For it did not happen without a purpose;
> And she did not require a midwife,
> For He [God the Father] delivered her.

So too Eusebius represents the Messiah as saying, "Thou thyself, my God and Father, as if playing the midwife's part, didst draw forth from the womb that flesh which had been prepared for me." Both these statements are probably derived from Psalm 22, commonly looked on as a Messianic prophecy by the Fathers: "Thou art he that took me out of the womb," where there is in reality no obstetrical idea, but merely the statement that man is born by God's help.

The *Protevangelium* goes on with the story of the visit of the Magi, the Flight into Egypt and the massacre of the Innocents. According to this story, when Mary heard that Herod's servants were searching for her son, she wrapped him in swaddling clothes and laid him in an ox-manger. Elizabeth, whose son, John the Baptist, was but little older than Jesus, and consequently in danger from Herod, fled with her baby into the hill country, and looked about for a hiding place. Finding none she cried out, "O mountain of God, receive a mother and her child!" and immediately the mountain broke open and took them in. But Herod sent to Zachariah to ask him where he had hidden his son, and when Zachariah answered that he did not know where John was, Herod had him put to death. Origen, however, gives a different account of the death of Zachariah. It was, he says, because he allowed Mary to serve among the virgins in the Temple, even after the Nativity.

We now come to the *Gospel of Thomas*, and the stories of the childhood of the Lord. Most of these stories have a recurring theme, not very creditable to Jesus. Another child runs into him, a teacher patronises him, a scribe rebukes him for breaking the Sabbath. Jesus is annoyed and strikes the offender dead. He sometimes, though not always, changes his mind and restores his victim to life. These unedifying stories become very monotonous; one or two on somewhat different lines may be told at greater length.

JESUS AND THE SPARROWS. One Sabbath day, when Jesus was five years old, a shower of rain had fallen, and he went out to where the water was running, and made little pools into which the water ran. And he spoke, bidding the water become clean and wholesome, and immediately it was so. Then he made some soft clay, and out of the clay fashioned twelve sparrows. One of his playfellows, who was watching, ran and told Joseph that his child was breaking the Sabbath. Joseph came out to see what was going on, and called out to him, "Why art thou profaning the Sabbath?" Jesus made no answer, but clapped his hands and cried out to the clay birds, "Go! and remember me!" And the sparrows rose up into the air and flew away chirping. And when Joseph saw it he was amazed.

JESUS AND THE DYER. One day the Blessed Virgin visited the house of a neighbour who was a dyer, and the child Jesus went with her. There were many vessels in the room containing coloured dyes, and various cloths which had been sent by different men to be dyed different colours. While Mary was talking to the dyer Jesus took all the different cloths, rolled them together and sank all of them in a vessel which contained nothing but a black dye.

When the dyer discovered what Jesus had done he was much vexed and complained to Mary, telling her she must make good the damage that her child had done. Mary rebuked her son gently, telling him he ought to be a cause of joy to her and not of grief. Jesus asked how he had grieved her. "By destroying this man's labour," she replied, "so that I must pay him for it." "How have I destroyed his labour?" asked the child, and Mary explained that each piece of cloth should have been dyed a different colour, but he had made them all alike black. When Jesus understood what he had done amiss he went to the vessel into which he had plunged the cloth and pulled each piece out, dyed a different colour, according to the wish of the dyer.

JESUS AND THE BROKEN PITCHER. When Jesus was six years old his mother sent him to fetch water, and gave him a pitcher to carry it in. But there were a number of people at the well, and one of them knocked up against his pitcher and broke it. So Jesus spread out his cloak and caught the water in it and brought it home to his mother.

HOW JESUS SOWED WHEAT. When it was time to sow, Jesus went out with his father to sow wheat in their field. And while Joseph was sowing, Jesus took one ear of wheat and sowed that. When harvest time came he reaped the corn that had grown up from the ear he had sowed, and threshed it, and made from it a hundred measures of wheat which he distributed among the poor. Jesus was eight years old when he performed this marvel.

JESUS AND THE BEAM OF WOOD. Another marvel performed by Jesus when he was eight years old was as follows. Joseph was a builder and a carpenter, who made ploughs and yokes for oxen. One day a rich man ordered from him a large, comfortable bed. But Joseph was troubled in his mind because the beam he had for the work was too short. Jesus, seeing his perplexity, said to him: "Be not troubled. Do you take hold of one end of the beam and I will take the other and we will pull it." This they did, and the beam was pulled out to the required length. When Joseph saw it he embraced the child and said, "God has blessed me in giving me such a son."

Another story of the childhood of Jesus is told in a curious Gnostic book belonging to the third century called *Pistis Sophia*. Its heretical character will at once be obvious. The Virgin Mary is represented as speaking to Jesus after the Resurrection.

"When thou wast a child, before the Spirit descended on thee, when thou wast in the vineyard with Joseph, the Spirit came down from the height and came unto me in the house. He was like unto thee and I knew him not, but thought he was thou. And he said unto me, 'Where is Jesus, my brother, that I may go to meet him?' And when he had said this I was in doubt and thought it was a phantom tempting me. I seized him and bound him to the foot of the bed which was in my house until I had gone to find you in the field, thee and Joseph. And I found you in the vineyard where Joseph was putting up the vine poles. It came to pass therefore that thou didst hear me telling this thing to Joseph, that thou didst understand and thou wert joyful and saidst, 'Where is he that I may see him? For I am expecting him in this place.' And it came to pass when Joseph heard thee say these words he was troubled.

"We went together, we entered the house and we found the Spirit bound to the bed and we gazed upon him and thee and found that thou wast like unto him. And he that was bound to the bed was unloosed; he embraced thee and kissed thee and thou didst kiss him, and ye became one and the same being."

The Gospel of Nicodemus

The Gospel of Nicodemus, sometimes called the Acts of Pilate, is a composite book, in two parts by different authors. The first part is ostensibly the official report of Christ's trial sent by Pilate to the Emperor. In some copies the Emperor is named Tiberius, in others Claudius.[1] The object of the book is to give incontrovertible evidence as to the truth of the Resurrection. It must not, however, be supposed that Justin Martyr was referring to it, when he tells the heathen that records of the trial will be found among the archives at Rome. He simply assumed that such records must exist. Early in the fourth century the Pagans produced forged *Acts of Pilate* directed against Christianity which were introduced into the schools by the orders of the Emperor Maximin. Some authorities suppose that the first part of the *Gospel of Nicodemus* was written to controvert them, but it may well be later. It contains an account of the attack by the Jews on Joseph of Arimathea for his part in the burial of Jesus, but it is not of great interest.

The second part—really a separate book, written, it is variously claimed, at any date between the second and fifth centuries—has a charm and an interest of its own. It contains a detailed narrative of the Descent of Christ and the Harrowing of Hell—that is, Christ's removal from hell of the patriarchs and saints of the Old Testament. The Harrowing of Hell was a favourite subject in the Middle Ages for poets and artists, and its popularity doubtless arose from a study of the *Gospel of Nicodemus*. This is not to be wondered at, for it is a delightful little work, composed and written with true literary art, rising in places to genuine eloquence.

The story is told by the two sons of the Simeon who received Jesus in the Temple and spoke over him the *Nunc Dimittis*.[2] After Christ's resurrection many saints rose from

[1] *V.* Irenaeus and the Gnostics, p. 133.   [2] Luke 2: 29-32.

their graves and wandered about the streets of Jerusalem.[1] At the same time Karinus and Leucius were found in Arimathea, having likewise risen from the dead. A deputation was sent to bring them to Jerusalem where they were questioned by Annas and Caiaphas, and urged to explain the manner of their resurrection.

"And when Karinus and Leucius heard this adjuration they trembled in their body and groaned, being troubled in heart. And looking up into heaven they made the seal of the cross with their fingers upon their tongues, and forthwith both of them spoke, saying: 'Give us each a volume of paper, and let us write that which we have seen and heard.' And they gave them to them and each of them sat down and wrote. . . ."

They tell how they and the Patriarchs were sitting together in the darkness of Hades when suddenly a glorious light shone upon them. The Patriarchs were immediately sure that this betokened the coming of the Messiah whom they had foretold. Satan and Hades consulted together as to what was to be done, when a voice cried . . . "Be ye lift up, ye everlasting doors, and the King of Glory shall come in." A violent earthquake took place which shook the earth above and broke open the gates of Hell. The damage done was seen by Dante, and Virgil told him it was caused at the moment of Christ's descent.[2] Thereupon "the Lord of Majesty appeared in the form of a man and lightened the eternal darkness and broke the bonds that could not be loosed. . . ." Christ delivered Satan into the power of Hades, summoned the Patriarchs around him and made them a short address. He then "stretched forth his hand and made the sign of the cross over Adam and over all his

---

[1] Matt. 27: 51-53.

[2] Ma certo, poco pria, se ben discerno
Che venisse Colui, che la gran preda
Levò a Dite del cerchio superno,
De tutte parti l'alta valle feda
Tremò sì, ch'io pensai che l'Universo
Sentisse amor. . . .

Dante. *Inf..* 12: 37-42.

66

saints, and he took the right hand of Adam and went up out
of Hell, and all the saints followed him. . . . And the Lord
holding the hand of Adam delivered him unto Michael the
archangel, and all the saints followed Michael, and he brought
them all into the glory and grace of paradise".

There they found Enoch and Elijah, who told them that
they had not tasted death, but would return in the last days
to Jerusalem to fight Antichrist.[1] In that great battle they
would be killed and after three days and a half would again
ascend on the clouds. The Patriarchs were then joined by the
Penitent Thief who had been admitted into Paradise on showing the sign of the cross to the angel on guard.

Karinus and Leucius and others of the saints were then sent
back to earth, and going down to the Jordan were baptised
and given white robes. After this all their companions were
caught up into the clouds, but they were told to remain for a
time and to continue in prayer.

"And when they had finished writing all these things in
the several volumes of paper they arose . . . and suddenly
they were transfigured and became white exceedingly, and
were no more seen."

The Correspondence of Jesus and Abgar

Perhaps the most astonishing story to be found in the
interesting *Ecclesiastical History of Eusebius* is concerned with
the correspondence between Our Lord and Abgar, King of
Edessa. Edessa was a town of North-Western Mesopotamia,
and Eusebius tells us that the official records of the city, containing the story, were still extant in his day.

Abgar the Black, King of Edessa, in the early years of the
first century A.D., suffered from a painful disease, incurable
by the local doctors. He sent one of his officials, Hannan,
keeper of the royal archives, to Rome, on a diplomatic mission

[1] Rev. 11: 3–12.

to the Emperor Tiberius. On his return journey Hannan passed through Jerusalem, where he saw Jesus, and was much impressed by his personality and the wonders he was performing. When he got back to Edessa he reported his impressions to the king, who was at once convinced that Jesus was either God or the Son of God. He therefore sent Hannan back to Jerusalem with a letter for Jesus, confessing his faith, and begging him to come to Edessa to cure him. In this letter, which Eusebius gives in full, he concludes by saying, "I hear that the Jews are mocking you and wish to ill-treat you. Now I have a city, very small and venerable, which is enough for us both."

Hannan arrived in Jerusalem on the Wednesday before the Passover, and found Jesus lodging in the house of Gamaliel, the High Priest. Jesus wrote a letter in reply to Abgar, which again Eusebius gives us in extenso.

"Blessed art thou who didst believe in me not having seen me. . . . Now, concerning what you wrote to me, to come to you, I must first complete here all the things for which I was sent, and then be taken up to Him who sent me. And when I have been taken up I will send you one of my disciples to heal your suffering, and give life to you and those with you."

Hannan knew that Abgar would be much disappointed at not seeing Jesus, so he obtained permission to paint his portrait, which he did with "very choice colours".

There are other accounts of how this portrait was made. John of Damascus (eighth century) says, "A tale is told how when Augusus (Abgar) was king over the Edessenes, he sent a portrait painter to paint a likeness of the Lord, and when the painter could not paint because of the brightness that shone from the countenance of the Lord, He Himself put a cloth over His own divine and life-giving face, and impressed on it an image of Himself" (de Fide Orthodoxa 14: 17). Again Constantine Porphyrogenitus (A.D. 959) tells us that Jesus wiped his face on a cloth, on his way to Calvary, and the imprint of his features was left on the cloth. Jesus delivered it to his disciple Thomas, who gave it to Thaddeus, the disciple sent to Edessa after the Ascension, according to our Lord's promise. An Arab historian (*c.* 944) informs us that when the Greeks were besieging Edessa they exchanged certain prisoners of war for the Edessan portrait and letter, which they took back to Constantinople. After Constantinople was taken by the Turks in 1453, the fate of these relics is uncertain. We hear no more of the letter, but the portrait is to be found both in the church of St. Sylvester in Venice, and the church of St. Bartholomew in Genoa. No doubt it was miraculously duplicated.

The story of the imprinted portrait will at once remind us of the well-known legend of Veronica, who, according to Mecarius Magnesia (fourth century) wiped the Lord's face when he was on his way to be crucified. This portrait is preserved at Rome, but as a rule only bishops are allowed to see it.

Eusebius has another story of a likeness of Jesus. Veronica or Bernice was by tradition the name of the woman who was cured by Christ of an issue of blood. Eusebius says that her house was well known. Outside it stood a brazen figure of a kneeling woman, stretching out her hands as a suppliant: opposite her was another figure of a man "clothed in comely fashion in a double cloak and stretching out his hand to the woman. At his feet on the monument itself, a strange species of plant was growing which climbed up to the border of the double cloak of brass and acted as an antidote to all kinds of diseases. This statue, they said, bore the likeness of Jesus". Eusebius goes on to say that there also exist painted portraits of Paul and Peter and of Christ himself.

Yet another portrait was said to have been made by the Magi, of the Infant Jesus, and this, too, is reported to have been taken by them to Edessa (Sp. Julius Africanus—*Events in Persia at the birth of Jesus Christ.*)

All these stories seem to have flourished chiefly among the unlearned—from the Fathers we hear little about them. Irenaeus says that the Gnostics claim to have a likeness of Christ "made by Pilate" (Contr. Haeres 1: 25), but he does not mention any genuine pictures. St. Augustine also, does not seem to be aware that reliable portraits were in existence, for in discussing the bodily appearance of the Lord he says "the countenance of the Lord Himself in the flesh is variously imagined ".

The letter, or at any rate copies of it, had a longer history. We hear of it from the pilgrim Etheria (or Silvia) who wrote an account of her travels probably towards the end of the fourth century. She went to Edessa, where she visited many memorable sacred places, but makes no mention of the portrait of the Lord. Nor does she seem to have seen the letter, of which she says she has many copies at home. She does, however, tell us that the bishop of Edessa described its talismanic powers. The Lord, said the bishop, had promised that no enemy should ever enter the town, and whenever it was attacked the letter was brought out and read at the gates, whereupon the enemy was always dispersed. It has also been found inscribed on the lintel of a church at Ephesus. During the Middle Ages its talismanic powers were known all over Europe—the Anglo-Saxons wore it as a phylactery which would protect them against lightning and hail, and perils by land and sea, by day and night and in dark places. Even as late as 1868 a local paper reports its use. "An old woman of Tillington Parish in Sussex keeps with religious care a printed copy of the apocryphal epistle of our Lord to Abgarus King of Edessa, which she bought from a pedlar, who told her that if she stuck it up on her kitchen wall it would preserve her and her home from witchcraft and the evil eye."

Apart from the letter and the portrait, the connection of the Lord with Edessa is curious, and if pursued will turn out to be extremely startling.

Eusebius tells us that Thomas sent Thaddeus to Edessa to cure and instruct Abgar. Who was this Thaddeus? He is named as one of the twelve Apostles, but Eusebius says he was one of the Seventy who were sent by the Lord to preach in the cities of Galilee. We have an apocryphal work in Syriac, called *The Doctrine of Addai*—obviously a variant of the name Thaddeus—which gives a full account of his mission and death. We shall have to return later to the question of his identity.

We must now examine the reasons for the connection of Thomas with Edessa. By tradition he was the Apostle of India, and we have an apocryphal work, *The Acts of Thomas*, giving a full account of his work there. But it appears certain that the mission in India must have originated in Edessa. In the *Clementine Recognitions* Peter says that at the moment Thomas is teaching in Parthia, and the *Acts of Thomas* clearly emanates from Edessa which indeed contained his relics, transported there from India.

On enquiry Thomas himself appears to be a somewhat enigmatical personality. He figures chiefly in St. John's Gospel, where he is introduced as "Thomas, called Didymus" (John 11: 16). But this is a curious statement, for Thomas is the Hebrew for twin, while Didymus is the Greek for it. It appears therefore as if the Evangelist were saying not "The Twin who is called the Twin" but "Thomas, in Greek Didymus", "Thomas, meaning Twin". The fact that Thomas has become such a common Christian name must not mislead us.

We must then ask whose twin he was, and what his real name was. We shall find the answer in the *Acts of Thomas*, where he is called Judas Thomas, and is said to be the twin of— Jesus! And this startling theory is not confined to the East. Isidore of Seville (seventh century) in *De Ortu et Obitu patrum* speaks of "Thomas the Apostle, Didymus of Christ, or in Latin twin (geminus) of Christ, and exactly like the Saviour". . . . This phrase was quoted in the *Legenda Sacrorum*, though the unorthodox words were eventually removed. Priscillian

(A.D. 385) also says "Judas the Apostle, claimed to be the Lord's twin". The *Acts of Thomas* are very emphatic on the subject of the twinship. A demon who has possession of an unfortunate woman asks Judas Thomas, "Why art thou like unto God thy Lord?" A colt who can miraculously speak hails him as "Twin of the Messiah". A girl is delivered from the place of torment by "Him who was like unto thee". Thomas visits a bride in her chamber, and when he leaves her the Lord himself appears, and the bride takes him for Judas Thomas. The Lord says, "I am not Judas, but I am the brother of Judas."

Judas of course is not Judas Iscariot, but Jude, called "the brother of the Lord" (Mark 6: 3), and also called Jude, author of the Epistle. This epistle begins, in our text, "Jude, the servant of Jesus Christ and brother of James." The Greek has an unnatural look: Ἰούδας Ἰησοῦ χριστοῦ δοῦλος ἀδςλφος δὲ Ἰακωβοῦ. It seems probable that the words δοῦλος and δὲ Ἰακωβοῦ have been interpolated in the interests of orthodoxy and that the primitive text ran Ἰούδας Ἰησοῦ χριστοῦ ἀδελφός —Jude, the brother of Jesus Christ.

It will have been noticed that Isidore of Seville has followed the *Acts of Thomas* in emphasising the likeness between the twins —one is often mistaken for the other. Now Judas Thomas, we are told, was a little man. When he was in a crowd "the people went up to lofty places that they might see him". With this should be compared the story of Zachaeus (Luke 19: 3). "He (Zachaeus) sought to see Jesus who he was, and could not for the press, because he was little of stature." This is quite ambiguous. The person who "was little of stature" might be Zachaeus or Jesus. It is always taken for granted that it was Zachaeus; but if Jesus was the identical twin of a very short man of course *he* must have been the one who was "little of stature".

The Fathers were divided in opinion as to the physical appearance of the Lord. The Church has always found a prophetic description of him in "The Suffering Servant" of

Isaiah. We are told (Isa. 53: 2, 3) "He hath no form nor come-liness, and when we shall see him there is no beauty that we should desire him. He is despised and rejected of men. . . ." This was often taken to mean that the Servant—and the Lord—were lepers, and there was a widespread belief that Jesus was indeed a leper. Not unnaturally the opposite view was held. He was of an imposing appearance—"very tall", says Ps. Lentulus, and very beautiful. Nicephorus has a curious passage. His description has the obvious intention of giving a portrait of a magnificent, glorious person, but he winds up "his height was fully seven spans"—which would be a little over five feet. These ideas were evidently widespread. Celsus, who wrote against Christianity in the second century, says, "The body of Jesus was, they say, small, ill-favoured and ignoble." Origen in his great work *Contra Celsum* writes at length to oppose this degrading description. "We admit that there are passages which speak of the body of Jesus as ill-favoured, but not ignoble . . .; nor is there clear evidence that it was small." Perhaps the true explanation is to be found in the apocryphal *Acts of John*: "He was often small and uncomely, and then again as reaching unto heaven." Origen supports this view. "How came Celsus," he says, "to overlook the fact that our Lord's body varied according to the capacity of the observers, and that a useful purpose was served when its appearance was such as was necessary for each individual?"[1]

It may easily be believed that the orthodox doctrine of the Virgin Birth caused the idea of the Lord's twin to be looked upon askance. The first trace of this is perhaps to be found in the *Acts of Thomas* where a Black Serpent, eventually overcome by Judas Thomas, declares, "I know the Ocean Flood of the Messiah will destroy us." Here Thomas is read as Tehom—the abyss or flood, instead of the common and correct *twin*. Another concession to the rising orthodoxy is to be found in the introduction of Thaddeus into the story of Edessa. The

[1] Cf. Acts of John, p. 106.

word Thaddeus has as a root the Hebrew for breast. Thaddeus is—not a twin, but a foster-brother—a *brust kind*, as the Germans say. The idea of an identical twin of the Messiah was becoming intolerable.

What was the reason for which these mysterious twins were connected with Edessa? Twins all over the world are early thought of as abnormal beings. Since it is obvious that a man can only beget one child at a time, what is more natural than to suppose that one of the children has a god for his father? This of course is the case with the most celebrated pair of twins —the Great Twin brethren, the Heavenly Twins. Zeus was the father of Pollux, who was an immortal, Tyndarus the father of Castor, who only attained immortality and a place in the sky by the affection of his brother. What were the characteristics of the Heavenly Twins? We all know they were tamers of horses, and they subdued storms, but they were also stonemasons and architects, carpenters, makers of ploughs and yokes, and at any rate when they appear as the Açvins in the *Rig Veda*, they cure diseases, give sight to the blind, and preside at wedding feasts. These are all characteristic of Judas Thomas in the *Acts of Thomas*. When the horses driving his chariot are worn out by fatigue Thomas summons a group of wild asses to his assistance and instructs four of their number to pull the chariot in their place. He describes himself as skilled in carpentry and architecture, a maker of ploughs and yokes and oars for ferry boats and masts for ships, and in stone a maker of tombstones and monuments and palaces for kings. When Thomas was in India the king, before going on a journey, gave him a large sum of money and ordered him to build a palace. But Thomas spent all the money in relieving the poor, and when the king returned there was no sign of a palace. Thomas explained that he had been building a palace for the king in heaven, but the king, naturally enough, was sceptical and ordered Thomas to be flayed and burnt alive. Fortunately for the Saint the king's brother died just at this time. He appeared to the king in a vision, and described enthusiastically the heavenly palace Thomas had built. So no more was said about flaying and burning. We have already mentioned the visit of Thomas to the bridal chamber of the Princess, to bless her and her young husband. A curious, remote connection between Thomas and the Heavenly Twins is his appointment of Xanthippus to be his successor. Now Xanthus was the name of one of the horses presented by Poseidon to Hera, and given by her to the Dioscuri.

It will be observed that many of these traits appear in the Gospel accounts of Jesus. He enters Jerusalem riding on a colt "whereon no man ever yet sat" (Mark 11: 2), so that he could obviously tame asses and horses. At Cana, where he performed his first miracle, he showed himself the patron of weddings. He gave sight to the blind. He had power to save ships in a storm—Thomas in his last sermon before his death tells his hearers that "in a storm Jesus will walk upon the waves of the sea and support your ship". This is the more noticeable as he is addressing an inland people, unacquainted with ships and seafaring.

The question of carpentry is a curious one. In the gospels it is mentioned twice. When Jesus is teaching in the synagogue in "his own country" the people, astonished at his learning, ask, "Is not this the carpenter?" (Mark 6: 3) or, according to Matthew, "the carpenter's son" (Matt. 13: 55). Matthew's version is perhaps due to a feeling that a carpenter's work is derogatory. Origen denies that he is called a carpenter in the gospels (*Contr. Cel.*), either forgetting Mark, or misreading it. In controversy the heathen often used the expression in scorn of the Christian's god. Simon Magus at Rome frequently sneered at Peter for worshipping a carpenter (Acts of Peter). An amusing story is told by Theodoret of Cyrrhus (*fl.* 450). He says that when Julian the Apostate was on his last expedition against the Parthians, a heathen asked a Christian contemptuously, "What is the carpenter's son doing now?" To which the Christian replied, "He is making a coffin." And sure enough, a few weeks later the Apostate was in need of a coffin. On the other hand the *Protevangelium*, the apocryphal *Gospel of the Infancy*, has a story already quoted of Jesus as a child lengthening a beam of wood by pulling at it, in order to help Joseph in his work. Justin Martyr hedges over the question. "When Jesus came to the Jordan and was supposed to be the son of Joseph the carpenter, and appeared without comeliness, as the Scripture had foretold and *was supposed* to be a carpenter (for these works of a carpenter were wrought by him when he was among men, namely ploughs and yokes) . . ." (Trypho 88). It will be noticed that the ploughs and yokes are the very things that Thomas claimed to be able to make.

We have now to enquire why the story of the Twins should have arisen in Edessa. It appears highly probable that there had long been a cult of the Dioscuri in this city—a cult that was in any case widespread over the East and indeed in the West as well. There are still standing on the site of Edessa two huge inscribed pillars, fifty feet high, which no doubt stood in front of a temple, most likely dedicated to the Dioscuri. We know that the Edessenes worshipped twin gods, whom they called Nebo and Bel, and there are many coins from the vicinity bearing on them two stars, a common symbol of the Heavenly Twins. It seems very likely that when Christianity was brought to Edessa the Church, instead of trying to abolish the old worship, substituted, as she so often did, a pair of Christian Twins for the heathen pair.

We must also mention that India in ancient astronomical thought was under the sign of the Zodiac Gemini. It was natural enough that the Gospel should be preached there by Thomas the Twin.

We have already pointed out that the development of theology made the idea of Jesus as a twin intolerable, and we have indicated some of the ways in which it was modified in the Edessan stories. A further example of this modification can be found in the Gospel itself. Mark, and Mark alone of the

Evangelists, tells us that Jesus named James and John, the sons of Zebedee, "Boanerges, which is, Sons of Thunder" (Mark 3: 17). The only other early writer to use the expression is Justin Martyr, who tells us that "in Peter's memoirs" it is recorded "that he changed the name of the sons of Zebedee to Sons of Thunder" (Dial. 106). Though the word *Boanerges* is a difficult one, which has puzzled all the commentators, it is clear that Mark was right in interpreting it Sons of Thunder, though perhaps he should have said *twin sons*. Here we have the Heavenly Twins again, this time most likely replacing the unwanted Jesus and Judas Thomas. The identification of the sons of Zebedee with the Great Twin Brethren is confirmed by the traditions concerning John, who was reputedly the Evangelist. A curious conversation between Jesus after the Resurrection and Peter is reported in the appendix to John's gospel, chapter 21.[1] Peter pointing to John asks the Lord, "What shall this man do?" To which the Lord replies, "If I will that he tarry till I come, what is that to thee?" and the narrative continues, " This saying therefore went forth among the brethren that that disciple should not die; yet Jesus said not unto him that he should not die but, If I will that he tarry till I come, what is that to thee?"

In spite of the ambiguous answer of Jesus, "the saying that went forth among the brethren" persisted. John did *not* die. Even in the days of St. Augustine it was believed "on the authority of 'a grave man' " that John was only sleeping in his grave and the earth could be seen to rise and fall as he breathed. Well, we know that one of the Heavenly Twins was a mortal —Herod killed James the brother of John with the sword (Acts 12: 1, 2)—but the other was one of the immortals.

The cult of the Great Twin Brethren may be traced in many cases of twin saints—Cosmas and Damian, the doctor saints, Florus and Laurus, the Russian patron saints of horses, and probably Crispin and Crispianus. On one occasion their part

[1] Now universally admitted not to be by the author of the Gospel.

was played by two saints, though they are not claimed as twins. In 394 Theodosius was about to give battle to Arbogastes, the murderer of Valentinian II. As he was setting forth at cockcrow he had a vision of two young men, dressed in white and mounted on white horses. They announced that they were St. Philip (of course connected with horses) and St. John—probably the brother of St. James, whose character as one of the gemini we already know. They announced that they had been sent to fight for Theodosius and bring him victory. In the ensuing battle, in which Theodosius was greatly outnumbered, the wind blew back the javelins and arrows discharged by the enemy, and blinded them with dust. Thus Arbogastes was defeated by the same divinities as had won the Battle of Lake Regillus.

> He was aware of a princely pair
> That rode at his right hand.
> So like they were that no one
> Might one from the other know—
> White as snow their armour was,
> Their horses white as snow.

Clement and the Clementines

One of the earliest Bishops of Rome, belonging indeed to the first century, seems to have been a certain Clement. He may have belonged to the family of Domitian, whose cousin Flavius Clemens died about A.D. 95. This Flavius was possibly a Christian, as his wife, Domitilla, Domitian's own niece, was banished, apparently on charges connected with Christianity. In any case Clement must have made an impression on the early church, for his name is connected with many writings, the real origin of which is for the most part unknown to us.

We have already dealt with the earliest of these writings, the *First Epistle of Clement to the Corinthians*.

The next work we come to is known as the *Second Epistle of Clement to the Corinthians*. Here we immediately leave the world of fact. It is not an epistle, but a homily. Both style and doctrine show it was not written by the author of the first Epistle and it was in all probability composed at least fifty years later—about A.D. 140.

The next writings we have to consider form a group by themselves. Though they still have the name of Clement attached to them they are clearly spurious, the romantic imaginings of some person or persons who wished to convey religious instruction in an attractive form, and under the authority of Clement of Rome. The most important of these writings is an epistle, obviously apocryphal, but supposed to be written by Clement to James, the brother of the Lord. It gives an account of how Peter, before his martyrdom, held a long discourse with Clement and then appointed him bishop in his place. We then take a further step into mystification with the *Clementine Homilies* and the *Clementine Recognitions*. These two books tell the same story of magic and adventure, sometimes in the same words, sometimes with slight variations. The story is embedded in a mass of doctrinal matter, also much alike in the two books. Who wrote them, which book came first, what relation they bear to each other and when they came into existence, are unsolved problems. They were originally in Greek but the *Recognitions* are extant only in a Latin translation made by Rufinus at the beginning of the fifth century. Beyond that little is known with certainty.

By omitting the theological and edifying discourses which make up the bulk of the books, and which were no doubt the cause of their being written, and by a little harmonising of the versions, the following curious tale has been extracted.

In the first century A.D. there lived in Rome a distinguished family, related to the Caesar, Domitian. The father was called Faustus, the mother Mattidia, and they had three sons—twins, Faustinus and Faustinianus, and a younger son Clement. One day Mattidia came to her husband in tears. She had, she said, had a terrible dream in which she had been warned that she must leave the city with the twin boys for ten years, or they would all be involved in ruin and death. Faustus was horrified by the news, but he did not hesitate. He arranged immediately for Mattidia to sail to Athens with the two boys, for whose education there she was to arrange. He gave her plenty of money and sent with her a number of slaves and servants, so that she should be well provided for. Clement, the youngest boy, he kept with him. After a year, having had no news of her, he sent messengers to Athens with money for her, but these messengers never returned. Two years later he sent more messengers, and these returned saying that Mattidia was certainly not in Athens, and that they were unable to obtain any news of her. Faustus was overcome with sorrow. He took Clement down to the port with him, and there made every possible enquiry, but he could get no news of his wife and children. He finally decided to go in search of her himself, and leaving Clement, now twelve years old, with trustworthy guardians, he set off. Clement never heard from him again, and after some years was sure that he must be dead.

As Clement grew up he became absorbed in the study of philosophy and religion. He was especially perplexed by such problems as the immortality of the soul, its pre-existence, the origin of the world and whether it would exist eternally or was doomed to dissolution. Though he frequented many different schools of philosophy he was convinced by none of them and he became more and more disquieted in his mind. The only teaching that at all appealed to him was that of the Jews, for he was naturally of a virtuous disposition, and their moral ideas seemed to him superior to those of the polytheists. He was still, however, oppressed by his inability to solve the philosophical doubts that obsessed him, and his mental distress brought on an illness which confined him to bed. While he was in this state he received a visit from one Appion,[1] an old friend of his father's. Finding Clement ill in bed he asked him what was the matter with him, for as he had some knowledge of medicine he might be able to help him. Now Clement knew that Appion hated the Jews and was violently opposed to their teaching. He therefore determined to play him a trick, and began by confessing that he was in love with a married woman who would have nothing to say to him.

"My son," replied Appion, "there is no cause for despair. I myself when young was in love with a woman I dared not even address. I fortunately fell in with an Egyptian who was well versed in magic, and when I had told him of my trouble he taught me an incantation by means of which I obtained my desire. This incantation I will teach to you, and within seven days you shall enjoy her you love."

"I do not altogether believe in magic," replied Clement, "and moreover even if your spell did work and I constrained a chaste woman against her will, I should fear a terrible punishment in Hades, along with Ixion, Tantalus, Sisyphus, and other adulterers. If however you could persuade her to come to me willingly I should be deeply grateful to you."

Appion was rather puzzled by Clement's attitude, but after a little he agreed to compose a letter in praise of adultery, which Clement should send her, and which would surely win her over. The letter was a long one, and contained a detailed account of the amours of the gods, and the arguments of the philosophers in favour of free love.

Clement took the letter and when Appion had left him he concocted another which was supposed to be the lady's answer. It denounced the stories of the gods as wicked fables and declared that she had learned from the Jews that there was but one God, who hated adultery and would punish those who indulged in it.

---

[1] This Appion is mentioned by Eusebius, *H.E.*, 2: 5, and again in connection apparently with the Clementines, 3: 38.

When Appion returned the next day Clement showed him the supposed answer.

"Ah," exclaimed Appion when he had read it. "Am I not right to hate the Jews? Some Jew or other has converted her to his religion, and I fear you will never be able to win her."

At that Clement confessed that the whole story of the love affair had been an invention and that his search for a true philosophy had led him to examine the Jewish religion, for which he felt much sympathy. Appion thereupon fell into a rage. He hated the Jews and did not know or want to know anything about their teaching. Indignant with Clement for his trick and his attitude towards the despised Jews, he left him in silence, and soon after quitted Rome.

Clement, however, continued his intercourse with the Jews, and soon a strange rumour reached his ears. It concerned a new teacher who had appeared in Judea. He was preaching the coming of the kingdom of God, and supporting his words with many signs and wonders, curing the sick, expelling demons, and even raising men from the dead. The report was soon followed up by the arrival of Barnabas, a disciple of the new teacher. He declared publicly that this teacher was the Son of God, and was promising eternal life to all those who believed in him and obeyed him.

Clement was much struck by this discourse, and defended Barnabas against hecklers who interrupted him with impertinent questions, such as "Why has a tiny creature like a gnat got six legs and two wings, whereas the ponderous elephant has only four legs and no wings at all?" Barnabas ignored the question and went on with his address, whereupon the unruly mob shouted rudely, and called him a barbarian and a madman. Clement intervened on behalf of Barnabas, and some of the bystanders came over to his view, while others remained obdurate. When evening fell and the preaching ended Clement took Barnabas by the hand and persuaded him to go home with him. Barnabas remained some days with

Clement, instructing him in true religion, but finally declared that he must return to Judea, which he would never leave, if he was to be subjected to such insults as he had received at Rome. Clement declared that he would follow him as soon as possible, and accompanying him to the port saw him on board a ship bound for Caesarea, and obtained from him instructions as to how to find his dwelling.

Clement kept his promise and arrived at Caesarea a fortnight later. As he went through the streets he heard the people talking with some excitement about a discussion that was to be held publicly, the following day, between Peter, a prominent disciple of the Man of Judea and Simon Magus, a Samaritan. On hearing this, Clement asked to be directed to Peter's lodging. As he stood outside the door Barnabas caught sight of him, welcomed him eagerly, drew him into the house and presented him to Peter. Peter received him most affectionately, and after thanking him for his hospitality to Barnabas at Rome, invited him to form one of the group who were travelling through Judea and Syria. Clement was delighted to accept this invitation, as he hoped to have his religious doubts set at rest by Peter's instruction. Nor indeed was he disappointed in this, for he was soon converted to the True Religion and baptised.

We must now give an account of the Simon Magus, with whom Peter was to have a disputation.[1] He was the son of Antonius and Rachel, both Samaritans, who worshipped on Mount Gerizim instead of at Jerusalem. He became an adherent of John the Baptist, who held him in high esteem, and intended him for his successor in the leadership of his sect. But Simon was away in Egypt studying magic at the time of John's death, and a certain Dositheus, who himself desired the first place, gave out that Simon was dead and thus was himself enabled to become the Standing One, as the head of the sect was called. When Simon returned from Egypt he did not openly oppose

---

[1] Acts 8. Though we are given a detailed account of Simon in the Clementines the story in Acts is not alluded to.

Dositheus, but accepted the second place, under him. He began however to undermine Dositheus's influence, saying that he was instructing his followers incorrectly owing to his ignorance of the true doctrine. This enraged Dositheus, who at one of their meetings struck Simon with his staff. But behold, a marvel took place—the staff passed through the body of Simon as if he had been smoke. Dositheus was thunderstruck, and asked Simon if he was the Standing One. Simon replied that he was, whereupon Dositheus, being well aware that he had wrongfully usurped the position, bowed down and worshipped him. A few days later Dositheus fell down and died, while Simon was accepted by all the sect as the Standing One. He claimed to have been born of a virgin, to have only the appearance of a man, being in reality a God. He travelled all over the land, preaching this wicked doctrine and performing false miracles.

This history of Simon was related by Peter to Clement, who was much astonished and begged for further information.

"There are two young men," replied Peter, "Aquila and Nicetas, who have been his followers for some time, and who can tell us much about him. Justa, the Canaanite woman, whose daughter was healed by the Lord,[1] was converted by Him to follow the Law of the Jews. In consequence of this her husband left her; but she bought two boys and adopted them as her own sons. They were educated with Simon Magus and are well acquainted with his teaching. But they have discovered his wickedness and deceit, and have now left him to follow us. They will tell you all you wish to know about him."

Peter then sent for the two young men, and when they arrived asked them to tell Clement what they knew about Simon.

Aquila, calling on God to witness that he spoke the truth, began as follows:

"For a long time, we who had been brought up with Simon

[1] Veronica or Bernice. *V.* p. 69.

believed him and followed his teaching. But at last we discovered his wickedness, and that he was actually a murderer. Before our very eyes, thinking we were his friends, he separated the soul of a boy from its own body by horrid incantations, and then, making an image of the child, set it up in the inner room where he sleeps. He explained to his followers that he had formed the body of the boy out of air, by divine arts, and they believed him; but we, who had seen his horrible ceremonies, knew he was a deceiver, denounced his impieties, and left him."

Then said Nicetas, "God is our witness that we never helped him in his wicked deeds though he made us many promises—that we should be worshipped as gods, honoured by kings, and enriched with boundless wealth, if we would keep his schemes secret. This we refused to do, and he became enraged with us, and threatened us with death if we revealed his mysteries and 'prodigies'."

Clement asked what the prodigies were, and the young men told him that he made statues walk, rolled himself in the fire without being burnt, flew through the air, transformed himself into a dragon, a goat, or a man with two faces, opened locked doors, melted iron, and produced phantom banquets at which the dishes seemed to come in of themselves, no bearers being visible.

Clement was now eager to be present at the disputation between Peter and Simon, which took place as arranged, in a public place, and lasted for three days. On the third day the question of the immortality of the soul arose—Simon denied it and Peter asserted it.

"You deny that the soul is immortal?" said Peter. "Go to your house, enter the inner chamber, and you will see an image clothed in purple—the image of a murdered boy. Ask him if the soul is immortal and he will inform you, for he knows."

At this Simon turned ashy white, for he was afraid that his house would be searched and the image found. He therefore assailed Peter with curses and blasphemies, attempting to cause a riot so that Peter's arguments should not be heard. But the onlookers were only roused to indignation against Simon; they drove him out, and only one man accompanied him in his flight.

The next day news reached Peter that Simon had left Caesarea at night, and betaken himself to Tyre. Peter determined to follow him, but he sent Clement, Aquila and Nicetas on in advance, that they might secretly keep a watch on Simon, and inform Peter as to his doings. When the three young men arrived in Tyre they took up their lodging with Bernice, the daughter of Justa, and adopted sister of Aquila and Nicetas. She received them hospitably and affectionately and invited them to stay in her house. They explained that the purpose of their visit was to spy on Simon Magus, and questioned her as to his doings in Tyre.

"Indeed," answered Bernice, "he has been performing many marvels since he arrived here and astonishes the whole city every day. He makes spectres and ghosts appear in the market-place and when he walks abroad shadows move before him, which he says are the souls of the dead. Some people denounced him as an impostor, but he contrived to pacify them and then offered them a banquet. For this banquet he killed an ox and when the visitors had eaten it he injected them with various diseases and caused them to be possessed by demons. In short, he is feared and honoured as a god, and I strongly advise you not to attempt to oppose him until you have Peter with you."

On learning this the young man sent off a letter to Peter informing him of the situation. The next morning they heard that Simon had left for Sidon, leaving three of his disciples behind. Taking a walk in the city they came upon these disciples and Clement was amazed to recognise among them the very Appion who had written the love-letter for him in Rome. Appion greeted him affectionately, and presented his two companions, Annubion and Athenodorus. He told them that Clement had forsaken his father's beliefs and the teachings of Greek philosophy, and been seduced by a barbarian called Peter to adopt the religion of the Jews. He invited Clement to discuss the question, and they had a long debate which lasted three days, at the end of which time neither had convinced the other. The next day Peter arrived from Caesarea, whereupon Appion, Annubion and Athenodorus withdrew.

Now began a long pursuit of Simon Magus by Peter and the three young men. They journeyed to Sidon, Beyrout, Byblus and Tripolis, always on the track of Simon, who constantly evaded them. At Tripolis they heard that Simon had gone to Antioch and Peter sent Aquila and Nicetas ahead, keeping Clement with him and travelling more slowly. Clement was delighted at being alone with Peter. Their intimacy and affection increased, and Clement confided to Peter his curious history, and how he had been separated from his father and mother and two brothers, and had abandoned any hope of their being alive. Peter wept in sympathy with Clement, but pointed out that had his father been a true believer people would have said his misfortunes were due to the anger of the gods—as he was a Gentile they attributed it to a malign fate.

By this time Clement and Peter had arrived at Antaradus, a city on the coast. A little distance off lay the island of Aradus on which there was a renowned temple, celebrated for its magnificent columns and beautiful wall paintings by Phidias. One of their company invited them to visit this temple, and Peter acquiescing they took a boat for the island. All the party entered the temple and admired the columns, and Peter, who was not interested in the wall paintings, then went out, leaving the others to examine the masterpiece of Phidias at their leisure.

As he came out of the temple Peter saw a poor woman

standing by the door, begging for alms from the passers-by. He stopped and spoke to her, asking her why she disgraced herself by begging, instead of working honestly for her living.

"Alas," replied the woman, "I cannot work. I have gnawed my hands until they are useless and as it were paralysed."

"What terrible sorrow caused you to do that?" asked Peter. "Tell me, and I will give you a drug that will enable you to live without distress."

The woman, not understanding that the drug he spoke of was the true religion, was pleased by his promise.

"My story is a strange one," she replied. "I come of a noble family and married a powerful man by whom I had three sons. I lived happily and virtuously, until a terrible misfortune befell me. My husband's brother, a wicked and unscrupulous man, fell madly in love with me, and began to pursue me with all the frenzy of unlawful passion. I was determined not to give way to him, but I did not wish to expose his wickedness to my husband, setting brother against brother, and bringing disgrace on the whole family. I decided it would be best for me to quit the city for a while with the two twins, leaving the third child behind to comfort his father. To achieve this without arousing my husband's suspicions, I told him I had been warned in a dream to depart with the two elder boys, lest we should all die miserably. My husband sadly agreed and sent us off by ship to Athens. But on the way the ship was wrecked in a terrible storm, not far from this island of Aradus. I was cast up on the rocks, all the rest of the ship's company as well as my two children were drowned, and I alone was rescued by the inhabitants of the island, who pulled me to shore and supplied me with food and clothes. One of the women, a poor widow, took me into her cottage; but my grief at the loss of my children was so great that I constantly gnawed my hands until they became powerless. Shortly afterwards the woman with whom I lived fell ill of a palsy and was confined to her bed. As we were both unable to work our only resource was for me to go out and beg; with what charitable passers-by give me I secure a scanty living for us both."

At that moment Clement came out of the temple and asked what Peter and the woman were talking about. Peter made no reply, but told Clement to enter the boat and wait for him there. When Clement had left them, Peter turned to the woman and said, "What is your family, O woman? From what city do you come, and what are the names of your husband and children?"

Now the woman was not willing to reveal herself. She therefore answered that she came from Ephesus, her husband from Sicily, and gave false names to her sons.

"Alas," said Peter, "I thought that some great joy was at hand for us: I suspected you were a woman of whom I have heard, whose tale resembled yours."

"Tell me about her, I adjure you," replied the woman, "that I may know if there is really anyone more unfortunate than I am."

"There is a young man with me, a Roman citizen," replied Peter, "who told me that his mother had had a vision which forced her to leave the city with her twin boys for fear of some terrible fate. She departed, and was never heard of again."

On hearing these words the woman gave a piercing cry and fainted. Peter went to her, supported her and spoke comforting words, asking her what was the matter. She turned her head towards him and asked faintly, "Where is that youth? I am his mother."

But Peter, to make assurance doubly sure, asked her, "What is his name? For if you do not tell me you shall not see him."

And the woman, with a sob of joy, cried out, "Clement!"

Peter, now convinced that she was indeed Clement's mother, spoke to her again.

"It is the same," he said, "and he is the youth who spoke to us just now, and is waiting for me on the ship. Come, we will join him." And taking her by the hand he led her down to the port.

When Clement saw them coming he went towards them and offered to support the woman instead of Peter. But as soon as he touched her she gave a great scream and seizing him in her arms, began to devour him with kisses. Clement, horrified by her behaviour, and taking her for a lunatic, pushed her away, and looked angrily at Peter.

"What are you doing, Clement?" cried Peter. "Do not push her away—she is your mother!"

At these words Clement gazed at the woman and recalled her appearance, and the longer he looked the more clearly he recognised her, until bursting into tears he put his arms round her and embraced her tenderly.

This, then, was the first RECOGNITION.

Peter now wished to sail away from the island of Aradus, but Mattidia turned to Clement, and said, "My darling son, I cannot leave without saying goodbye to the woman who took me in, for she is old, and paralysed and bed-ridden."

Peter commended her for her kind thought and ordered some of the sailors to bring the poor woman down to the ship. They carried her down on her bed, and Peter, looking up to heaven, prayed that she might be cured; and immediately she rose from her bed, fell down at Peter's feet and asked what it all meant. Mattidia told her the whole story briefly and then, having seen Peter's miraculous powers, begged him to restore to her the use of her hands. He placed his hands on hers and she was cured and the two women embraced each other with tears. Clement then presented a thousand drachms to his mother's hostess and committed her to the charge of the chief man of the town, who willingly consented to look after her. When all these matters had been satisfactorily concluded, Peter, Clement and Mattidia set sail for Antaradus.

When they arrived at their lodging Mattidia asked Clement what had become of her husband. He told her that Faustus had set out to look for her but had never returned, whereupon she sighed deeply, but made no lament; her joy at having recovered one of her sons lightened her other sorrows. The next morning, by Peter's orders, his wife, Mattidia and Clement took their seats in a waggon that was waiting for them and set off towards Caesarea, which they reached next day, Peter following on foot. At the gates of Caesarea Aquila and Nicetas met them, and conducted them to their lodging. Aquila and Nicetas asked who the strange woman was, and Clement replied that she was his mother, whom Peter, by God's help, had restored to him. At their request Peter gave them an account of all that had happened at Aradus and ended by telling them that Mattidia's twin boys were called Faustinus and Faustinianus.

At that Aquila and Nicetas sprang up in great agitation, and exclaimed, "O Lord and Ruler of the universe, is this true, or is it a dream?"

"Unless we are mad," replied Peter, "it is all true."

Then the young men cried out, "We are Faustinus and Faustinianus! When you began your story we suspected it was so, but we waited till the end, until we were certain that it was indeed of our family that you were speaking." Then they rushed in great excitement into their mother's room, and found her asleep. They would nevertheless have embraced her, but Peter restrained them, for fear the sudden shock of joy should unhinge her reason. "Let me," said he, "prepare her mind for this new and unexpected happiness."

Shortly afterwards Mattidia awoke naturally from her sleep, and Peter said to her, "I must tell you, O woman, that those who wish to join our religion must first be immersed three times and consecrated in holy water. Before this baptism they may not eat with us, not even if it were a father or a mother. For this reason I hope you will not think it hard that your son Clement cannot take his meals with you."

"But," exclaimed Mattidia, "what hinders me from being

baptised? Long ago I turned from the heathen gods; I have always lived chaste and pure even in the days of my greatest poverty. And I lament, not so much that my twins were drowned, as that they were lost, body and soul, before they learned the true religion."

At these words the two brothers could contain themselves no longer, but flinging their arms round their mother they embraced her with many tears.

"What is the meaning of this?" asked Mattidia, in great astonishment.

"Have courage," replied Peter, "and prepare for new joy. These are your sons, Faustinus and Faustinianus, who you thought were drowned. How they escaped, and why they are now called Aquila and Nicetas, I do not know. They will tell you themselves and we shall hear it along with you."

On hearing this Mattidia fainted from excess of emotion, and after a short time, when she came to herself she besought her sons to tell her what had happened to them.

"On that night, my mother," began Nicetas, "when the ship was broken up by the storm, we clung to pieces of wreckage and managed to keep afloat. We were rescued from this extreme peril by some men who turned out to be pirates. They put us into their boat and carried us to Caesarea. There they starved us, beat us and terrorised us, threatening us with horrible vengeance if we should betray them. They changed our names and sold us to a Canaanite woman called Justa. But she was an honourable and virtuous woman, who had been converted to the Jewish religion, and she treated us like her own sons and had us carefully educated in Greek literature and philosophy. How we were at first led astray by the sorcerer Simon Magus, and how we discovered his impostures and finally learnt the true religion from Peter, we will tell you at a more convenient time."

This, then, was the second RECOGNITION.

When Mattidia had heard Nicetas's story she fell down

at Peter's feet and begged him to baptise both her and the widow who had befriended her, that very day: that she might not spend a single day without her sons' companionship.

"That is impossible," replied Peter. " Before baptism the postulant must fast. As you have shown great charity in asking that your benefactress may be baptised as well as you, one day's fast will be sufficient, otherwise your purification must have lasted several days."

"Indeed," cried Mattidia, "I call God to witness that since I recovered my son excess of joy has prevented me from breaking my fast, except that yesterday I drank a cup of water."

Peter's wife, who had been with her all the time, vouched for the truth of her statement, and Aquila called out joyfully, "What then hinders her from being baptised?"

But Peter, smiling, shook his head.

"This was not a fast in preparation for baptism," he said mildly, "but what might be called an accidental fast. We will all fast with her, for one more day, and then she shall be baptised and enter into our communion."

Thus was it done. The next day they took Mattidia down to the sea, where she was duly baptised, and on returning to their lodging was initiated into all the mysteries of the true religion.

The day after the baptism Peter took the three brothers down to the sea, and after bathing they went to a retired spot where they could pray unobserved. But an old man, in workman's clothes, watched them, unperceived by them. He saw them praying, and waited till they had finished and come out from their retreat. He then approached, saluted them, and asked if he might have speech with them. His manner was grave and dignified, and Peter assured him that they would be glad to hear what he had to say. The old man then explained that he was sorry for them. He had observed them at prayer and pitied their error. "For," said he, "there is no God, no Providence, and you can obtain nothing by prayer. Whatever is written in the stars will inevitably come to pass; nothing can alter the fore-ordained sequence of events. I am myself profoundly learned in the science of astrology, and I can assure you that this is undoubtedly true."

Clement felt a strange stirring at his heart while the old man was speaking and he interrupted to ask who the old man was and what was his family.

"What has that to do with the matter in hand?" replied the old man. "Let us first discuss the question of prayer and fate—afterwards we can talk to each other in friendly fashion about our families."

Peter, who did not despise the old man for his poverty-stricken appearance, but respected him for the gravity of his manner and the kindliness of his proposal, agreed to a discussion. The discussion was a long one—in fact it lasted three days, and attracted a large number of the citizens of Caesarea to listen to it. On the first day Nicetas maintained the argument, on the second Aquila and on the third Clement. Now all this time the old man, though he spoke courteously and commended the eloquence and arguments of his opponents, remained firmly of opinion that all things were ruled by fate, and that prayers were of no avail. On the third day Clement pressed him hard and at last the old man said, "I know from my own experience that our future lives are inexorably fore-ordained for us. I took the horoscope of my wife, and found that she had Mars and Venus above the centre, the Moon setting in the house of Mars and the confines of Saturn. Now this configuration leads women to be adulteresses, to love their own slaves, and to end their days in foreign travel and by water. And so it happened to my wife. She fell in love with her slave, fled with him, and having satisfied her love perished in the sea."

" How do you know," asked Clement, "that she cohabited with her slave and died by drowning?"

"I know it with absolute certainty," replied the old man, "for after she had fled, my brother told me the whole story.

She had first made love to him but he had refused to listen to her. She, therefore, fearing lest my brother should reveal her attempt to me, pretended to have had a dream in which she was warned to flee from the city, taking with her her two twin sons. I immediately sent her away with the children, keeping only our youngest son with me."

The three young men, perceiving what a revelation was about to be made, could not restrain their tears. But Peter silenced them.

"What was the name of your younger son?" he asked.

And the old man replied, "Clement."

"Now," said Peter, "if I this day restore to you your wife, a chaste and virtuous woman, and your three sons, will you believe that unreasonable desires can be resisted and that there is a God who answers prayer?"

"As it is impossible for you to do this," replied the old man, "so it is impossible for anything to take place that is not fore-ordained."

Peter then turned to the listening crowds, and said, "Hear now what I have to say. This man, who looks so poor and wretched, is a citizen of Rome, of the family of Caesar. His name is Faustus, and he married a woman of high rank called Mattidia. His twin sons were called Faustinus and Faus-tinianus, his youngest son Clement, and moreover——" And here he pointed in turn to the three young men beside him—"this youth is Clement, this one, known as Aquila, is Faustinus, and this one called Nicetas is Faustinianus."

When Peter pronounced the names of his sons the old man was so overcome that his limbs would not support him. The young men rushed to embrace him, and when he was somewhat revived, and the amazement of the crowd was abating, Peter told more at length the story of the family and how they had come to be recognised. While he was still speaking, Mattidia, to whom the news had been carried by one of the spectators, rushed forward crying, "Where is my husband, where is my lord Faustus?" As she continued shouting like one demented, and gazing wildly round her, the old man ran towards her, and clasped her in his arms.

This then is the third RECOGNITION. But the story is not quite finished.

While these matters were in progress Simon Magus, accompanied by Appion, Annubion and Athenodorus, had been preaching against Peter in Antioch. He persuaded the crowd that Peter was a magician and a murderer, and roused them to such a frenzy of hatred against him that they were thirsting for his blood. The friends of Peter, much alarmed by the dangerous mood of the people, held a secret conclave to discuss what ought to be done. It so happened that Cornelius the Centurion[1] had arrived in the city on public business. Peter's friends approached him and asked whether he could do anything to help them to get rid of Simon. He readily promised to do so, and explained the plan that he had formed. Caesar, he said, had issued an edict that sorcerers both in Rome and the provinces were to be destroyed, and many had already been put to death. Cornelius would give out that he had been sent by Caesar to enforce this edict. If they could let Simon hear of this he would certainly be terrified and take to flight. The friends of Peter fell in with this scheme, and it was not long before Simon fled with his friends to Laodicea, where Peter by this time was established.

Meanwhile Faustus, staying in Peter's lodging with his newly-found family, was undergoing further instruction, and gradually coming nearer and nearer to a right belief. One evening some men from Antioch visited Peter and told him how Simon and his friends had been frightened away from Antioch, and were now in Laodicea. When Faustus heard this he was much pleased, for he was an old friend of Appion and Annubion, and much desired to see them. He asked Peter if there was any objection to this and Peter replied that on the

[1] Acts 10.

contrary he was much to be commended for his loyal affection for his friends. Faustus therefore went off to visit them. Towards daybreak they began to wonder why he had not returned, when to their horror the door opened and Simon Magus walked in. They shrank from him with repulsion and began to curse him, whereupon Peter asked them indignantly why they cursed their father. It then became apparent that it was indeed Faustus who stood there, but he had the face of Simon, though he retained his own voice. Peter was the only one among them to whom his face appeared unchanged.

"It is clear to me," said Peter, "what has happened. Simon is afraid of being arrested as a sorcerer, and he has put his face on you that you may be seized and put to death in his place. This he has doubtless done to be revenged on Aquila and Nicetas, whom he cannot forgive for having deserted from him."

"It is true, it is true," cried Faustus in great agitation, "for Annubion, who is very friendly towards me, warned me of his magic deceptions, but I would not believe him."

At this all the family burst into lamentation, Mattidia weeping most of all, and tearing her dishevelled hair. While they were in this great distress Annubion entered to tell them that Simon had fled during the night towards Judea. Seeing the misery on the faces of all around him he gazed at them dumbfounded. Peter again attempted to reassure the wretched family. He protested that the man who stood there would surely be restored to his own appearance by God, for he was really and truly their father.

"Indeed he is," said Annubion, "and I will tell you how it happened. We were standing talking to Simon, who was telling us of how he had been driven from Antioch and did not even dare to stay in Laodicea, when Faustus came in. Simon led us aside and told us to ask him to supper. 'Meanwhile,' said he, 'I will prepare an ointment with which he shall anoint his face after supper, and from that time he will appear exactly like me. But you, wash your faces in this juice, and you will not be deceived by the change. Thus, if he is caught he will be put to death as a sorcerer, and I shall be revenged on the traitors, Aquila and Nicetas.' Simon gave me no opportunity for speaking to Faustus privately, and warning him of this horrible plot. And now Simon has made off towards Judea, taking Appion and Athenodorus with him. I feigned illness, to avoid going with them, and made haste to visit Faustus, to see how things were with him."

"Now," said Peter, "we will take advantage of the malicious trick that Simon has played. You, Faustus, must go to Antioch, accompanied by Mattidia. When you are there, and everyone takes you for Simon, you must stand in the market place and announce that you have come in a repentant spirit to confess your sins. You must say that all that you spoke against Peter was false—he is neither a seducer, nor a murderer, nor a magician, but a holy man, a disciple and apostle of the true Prophet. Tell them you know all this from an angel of God who appeared to you in the night and rebuked you and scourged you terribly for your sins. And you must acknowledge that you are a wicked magician who has done nothing but evil all his life."

Faustus at once replied that he fully understood what he was to do, and would carry it out to the letter.

"When you have done all this," said Peter, "and have turned the minds of the people towards me, send for me. I shall come immediately, and give you back your own face."

It is hardly necessary to say that all fell out as Peter had anticipated. Such was the vehemence with which Faustus praised Peter and denounced himself that the people of Antioch could hardly be restrained from tearing him to pieces. He managed to hide until he had recovered his own face, and was ready to welcome Peter, who made a triumphal entry into the city. Faustus declared that he now fully recognised the truth of Peter's teaching and begged to be allowed to enter the spiritual circle of the true believers. Thus, after so many misfortunes and such marvellous vicissitudes, the whole family was reunited, and, let us hope, lived happily ever afterwards.

Simon Magus at Rome

There is a sequel to the story of the *Clementine Recognitions*. After Simon had been confuted and exposed by Peter in Palestine he fled to Rome. Peter followed him and the contention was resumed. The story of this second struggle is mainly to be pieced together from various apocryphal writings, the chief of which are *The Acts of Peter* and *The Passion of Peter and Paul*.

One day Simon appeared mysteriously in Rome, having apparently flown down from the sky. This miraculous appearance, followed as it was by a series of magical performances, impressed the people so much that they began to worship him as a god.[1] But shortly afterwards he was followed by Peter who immediately began to expose his deceitful pretensions, and to counteract his bogus tricks by genuine miracles. Simon was lodging in the house of a certain Marcellus, and Peter, followed by a crowd of curious persons, presented himself at the door and told the porter to fetch Simon out. This the porter refused to do. Simon, he said, had had foreknowledge of Peter's arrival and had ordered the porter to deny that he was in the house. At the door there was a large and powerful dog, fastened by a strong chain. Peter unloosed the dog, which immediately spoke in a man's voice, saying, "What do you order me to do?"

"Go into the house where Simon is sitting," replied Peter, "and tell him in front of the company to come out and speak to me."

The dog immediately rushed into the house, where Simon was surrounded by his admirers, lifted up his fore-feet and

[1] *V*. Justin Martyr, p. 44.

cried in a loud voice, "Peter commands you to come out
and speak to him, O wicked deceiver, for it is on your account
that he has come to Rome." The assembled company were
filled with amazement, and Simon himself could for the
moment find no words with which to answer. But the host,
Marcellus, immediately realised that Simon was an impostor.
He hurried out, flung himself at Peter's feet, confessed that he
had been led astray and begged for forgiveness. Peter received
him kindly and embraced him; but while he was speaking to
him one of the bystanders gave a cynical laugh. Peter perceived
that this was the voice of an evil spirit, and called out, "Come
forward, whoever it was that laughed!"

A young man ran out from the crowd and dashed himself against the wall of the house, crying out, "There is a
great dispute going on between the dog you sent and Simon,
for the dog has more to say than what you charged him
with."

Peter cried out in a loud voice, "Come out of the young
man, devil, whoever you are, and do him no injury."

Now outside the house was a great marble statue of Caesar.
When the young man heard Peter's command the devil
within him caused him to seize hold of the statue, throw it
to the ground and break it in pieces. Marcellus was terrified.

"This is a great crime," he said, "and if it is reported to
Caesar we shall all be terribly punished."

But Peter was undisturbed; at his bidding Marcellus took
some water in his hands, sprinkled it over the broken statue,
and at once it became whole as it had been before.

Meanwhile Simon and the dog were having a great argument. Simon ordered the dog to tell Peter he was not in the
house, while the dog asked Simon how he dared defy Peter
and cursed him as a corrupter of the truth and an enemy of
God. Eventually the dog left the house and reported his
conversation with Simon. He ended by making a solemn
announcement. "Peter," he said, "you and Simon will have a

great contest. You will turn many to the true faith, and receive from God the reward of your work."

With these words he fell down at Peter's feet and gave up the ghost.

The crowd were much impressed by these doings, and some of them called out to Peter to show them more signs, for Simon, they said, had performed many wonders and for that reason they had followed him.

Peter turned round and saw a fishmonger's shop with fish hanging in the window. He took a herring out of it and threw it into a bathing pool that was near at hand. Immediately the herring came to life and began swimming about. It was clearly no false apparition, for it continued swimming for a long time, and many people came to see it, some of them throwing it pieces of bread which it ate.

Meanwhile Marcellus went back to his house, where Simon was sitting alone at the dining-table, and covered him with abuse. He ordered his slaves to drive him out of the house and they fell upon him violently; some struck him in the face, some beat him with sticks, some stoned him and some poured filth over his head. Simon fled in disorder and ran to the house of Narcissus a presbyter, with whom Peter was lodging. He stood at the gate and called out, "I am here, I, Simon. Come down, Peter, and I will convict you of worshipping a Jew, a carpenter's son."

When Peter was told of this he turned to a woman who was suckling her seven-months infant.

"Go down quickly," he said to her, "to the man who is asking for me. There will be no need for you to speak at all, only listen to what your child says." And when the woman stood at the gate where Simon was waiting the infant spoke with a man's voice.

"O wretch abhorred by God," he cried, "sower of corruption, destroyer of truth, son of Satan destined to eternal punishment, you were not confounded when a dog rebuked you—hear now what I, an infant, compelled by God, have to say. On the next Sabbath, in the forum of Julius, you shall meet a man who will expose your deceit and wickedness. Until that time be stricken dumb, and depart from the city of Rome."

At these words Simon found that he was indeed unable to speak, and he left Rome and hid himself in a stable.

During the days before the time appointed for the disputation with Simon, Peter went to stay at the house of Marcellus. Marcellus had purified the house from all traces of the evil brought in by Simon, sprinkling the rooms, the porticos and the outer gate with holy water. He called together a number of virtuous widows and old women, and Peter preached to them and performed a series of healing miracles, in particular curing several of them of blindness.

When the Sabbath day had come a vast crowd collected in the Theatre of Julius, many paying as much as a piece of gold for their places. The meeting was presided over by the prefect of the city and Nero the emperor himself was present. When Peter and Simon stood face to face the discussion began, with a good deal of personal abuse, and Peter defied Simon then and there to perform a convincing wonder. Simon asked permission from the prefect, who wishing to be quite impartial put forward a young slave of his, and desired Simon to kill him and Peter to restore him to life. Simon at once stepped forward and whispered in the boy's ear, who immediately fell down dead. Peter then turned to the prefect, who was somewhat perturbed by the death of his slave, and told him to go to the boy and take his right hand. The prefect ran forward, took the boy's hand as he had been told, and the boy recovered his life, stood up, and walked. The audience acclaimed Peter and shouted out, "God is one, the God of Peter is one!" and a widow woman who had been present begged Peter to restore to life her son too, who had recently died. Peter told her to have him brought in, and a group of young men came forward, bearing the body on a bier. Peter then turned to Simon, and asked him if he could restore life, as well as take it away. Simon hesitated for a moment and then, approaching the bier, stooped over it, and said three times, "Raise thyself." Thereupon the young man lifted his head, opened his eyes and bowed slightly towards Simon. The crowd now shouted applause for Simon, but Peter said, calmly and coldly, "If he is really alive let him stand up and walk. This is merely a piece of sorcery, and if Simon moves away from the bier you will see that the young man is as dead as ever."

On hearing this the prefect pushed Simon away from the bier with his own hands, and sure enough the corpse was a corpse as before. Peter then touched his side and said, "Arise." And he arose, put off his grave clothes, came down from the bier, and confessed his belief in the Lord.

At this point Nero intervened. He had previously been convinced that Simon had divine powers, and allied himself with the deceiver.

"There is no doubt," he said, "that Simon is God, for he performed a conclusive miracle. His head was cut off by the executioner, and he rose again the third day."

"I know nothing about that," replied Peter, "for I was not present." The true explanation, which afterwards came to light, was that in the darkness of the execution-room Simon had substituted the head of a ram for his own head, and the executioner was too much frightened to reveal the fraud.

"If he is really God," Peter continued, "he will be able to tell my thoughts, for God alone knows the secrets of men's hearts."

"I will summon my angels to my help," cried Simon defiantly.

Peter now concealed in his sleeves two loaves of barley bread, which had been blessed and cut in halves. Simon in a fury caused the apparition of two enormous, fierce dogs, who precipitated themselves on Peter. He held out the loaves of holy bread to them and they immediately disappeared. Peter had thus proved that he had read Simon's thoughts, for of course the angels he had said he would summon were demons in the shape of the two dogs, so easily put to flight by Peter.

The end of Simon is told in various ways. Hippolytus, writing probably shortly after the *Acts of Peter*, says that he seated himself under a plane tree, and after preaching lies to the people declared that if he was buried alive he would rise again the third day. "So," says Hippolytus, "his disciples dug a grave and buried him in it, where he remains to this day. For he was not the Christ."

Most of the stories, however, tell us that Simon boasted that he would fly to heaven. A great crowd assembled to witness this marvel, and sure enough he rose in the air and appeared to be ascending. But Peter uttered a powerful prayer to God. His evil powers abandoned Simon, who crashed to the ground and was either killed immediately or was so badly injured that an operation became necessary and he died under the surgeon's knife.

These stories are evidently of the nature of folk-lore, and are interesting from the fact that they were so widely spread and believed by ordinary people in the early days of the church, and even in the Middle Ages. What truth underlies them?

There is no reason to believe that the meeting between Peter and Simon recorded in Acts[1] is not true. There was also in the first centuries of the Christian era an heretical sect of Simonians claiming to be followers of Simon. Eusebius says that Simon was the first author of heresies. His followers, he tells us, "prostrate themselves before statues of Simon, and worship them with incense, sacrifices and libations." "Their more secret rites . . . are full of marvel and frenzy and madness; for they are of such a kind that not only can they not be related in

[1] Acts 8.

writing—they are so full of baseness and unspeakable conduct that they cannot even be mentioned by the lips of decent men." He goes on to speak of "the utter foulness of the heresy of these men, who make a mocking sport of wretched women, 'weighed down', as is truly said, by every kind of evil."

Such accusations of gross immorality are constantly made by the orthodox against heretics—and, we may add, by heretics against the orthodox. They may, or may not, be founded on fact. Eusebius goes on to say that after "he had been detected in his crimes in Judea by the Apostle Peter" Simon went to Rome where he had great success and attracted many followers. Eusebius, however, says nothing of the contest in supernatural displays between Simon and Peter.

Many other early fathers speak—somewhat vaguely—of the disputes between Simon Magus and Peter at Rome, but the miraculous element is not emphasised. The *Acts of Peter*, from which our account is chiefly derived, were indeed formally condemned by Leo the Great (*c.*A.D. 450), but they continued to be read and enjoyed by many, and were thereafter repeatedly condemned, in vain. Their popularity continued, as we have said, throughout the Middle Ages.

The Acts of John

The *Acts of John*, belonging to the middle of the second century, afford a good example of a Gnostic and docetic composition. The writer expatiates at great length on the wickedness of any sexual intercourse and he depicts John as a pure virgin who throughout his life abstained from all fleshly contact with women. Many of John's miracles consist in bringing to life dead persons, whom he converts to Christianity, and whom even when they are married he persuades to live in future as celibates. This would not of itself necessarily be heretical, for a similar doctrine was taught by many who were strictly orthodox, though the *Acts of John* certainly carries the teaching to strange lengths. But his views on the person of Christ are darkly tinged with docetism. The body of the Lord was by no means that of an ordinary man, for its appearance changed entirely at different times, and even at the same time to different people.

In one of the many sermons John is reported to have preached he endeavours to explain this mystery, which he truly declares is incomprehensible.

"For when he had chosen Peter and Andrew to be his disciples he came to me and my brother James saying, 'I have need of you; come to me.' And my brother said, 'What does this child want, standing on the sea shore and calling to us?' And I said, 'What child?' And he replied, 'The one that is beckoning to us.' And I answered, 'Because of our long watch at sea your sight is troubled. Do you not see a man standing there, comely and fair, and with a cheerful face?' But he could see nothing but a child."

The two brothers took their ship to land, and the mysterious figure helped to moor it. But now John saw him as a man with a bald head and a flowing beard, and James as a youth whose beard was only beginning to grow. These changes in the Lord's appearance were continual. Sometimes he seemed short and plain, at other times he seemed to reach to heaven. When John leant upon his breast at meal-times sometimes it was smooth and tender and sometimes hard as stones. Once when John stood behind him, looking at his hinder parts, he was seen to be quite naked, his feet whiter than snow and lighting up the ground he stood on, and his head touching the sky. John never saw him wink—his eyes were always fully open, nor did he leave any foot-prints where he trod. All this was perplexing, and disturbed the minds of the disciples. On one occasion the Lord said to John, "Go to sleep." John pretended to be asleep, but secretly watched from under his mantle. He saw another Being, exactly like the Lord, approach, and heard him say, "Jesus, they whom thou hast chosen do not yet believe in thee." And the Lord replied, "Thou sayest true; for they are men."

The sermon continues with the description of a strange scene on the Mount of Olives just before the Betrayal. Jesus calls together all the apostles and bids them take hands and stand in a circle around him. They all dance together while Jesus sings a mystic hymn, the apostles always answering *Amen*. This hymn, full of gnostic symbols and sacred numbers, is too long to give in its entirety, but a few lines may be quoted.

Glory be to thee, Father.
    (*The apostles answer:*)   Amen.
Glory be to thee, Word.   Amen.
Glory be to thee, Grace.   Amen.

Grace danceth. I would pipe; dance all of you. Amen.

The number Eight singeth praise with us.   Amen.
The number Twelve danceth with us.   Amen.
The Whole on high hath part in our dancing.   Amen.

I would save and I would be saved.   Amen.
I would be wounded and I would wound. Amen.
I would eat and I would be eaten.   Amen.

Now answer thou unto my dancing.

The strange medley continues in the same strain, all dancing together, until at last the Lord departs. But, John adds, when the time for the Crucifixion arrived, he could not stay to see him suffer, but fled away and hid in a cave of the Mount of Olives. Then at the sixth hour darkness covered all the earth; when suddenly the Lord was standing in the cave, filling it with light. And he said, "John, to the multitude below in Jerusalem, I am being crucified and pierced: and gall and vinegar is given me to drink. But to thee I speak; hear thou what I say. . . .

Thou hearest that I suffered, yet I did not suffer; that I was pierced, yet I was not smitten; . . . that blood flowed from me, and it did not flow."

All this tallies with the teaching of Basilides (*fl. c.* 130), explained by Irenaeus in his book on docetic heresies, an account of which will be found later on.[1]

Interwoven among these heterodox teachings there are a number of anecdotes, which somehow leave an impression of a real man—kind-hearted, singularly ingenuous, and not without a sense of humour.

A certain Lycomedes, whom John had raised from the dead, had a friend who was a painter. It struck him that it would be delightful to have a portrait of the holy man. Lycomedes therefore placed the painter in a room from which he could see into another apartment where John and Lycomedes were conversing. On the first day the painter made an outline of John; on the next he painted in the colours and delivered the completed portrait to Lycomedes, who received it with great joy. He made a little shrine for the picture in his bedroom, and constantly went in to gaze at it. John noticing his behaviour asked him with a smile whether he was keeping something secret from him, and following him into his bedroom saw the portrait of an old man with garlands hanging on it and lamps and altars set before it. John was much startled at the sight, and asked Lycomedes if this was one of his gods. Lycomedes replied, "My only God is he who raised me from death; but if it be right that next to God the men who have benefited us should be called gods—it is thou, father, whom I have had painted in that portrait, whom I crown and love and reverence, as having become my revered guide."

At this John, who had never seen his own face, declared he did not believe the portrait could be like him, and accused Lycomedes of laughing at him. So Lycomedes brought a mirror, and John looked at his reflexion and compared it with

[1] *V.* Irenaeus, p. 130.

the portrait, and admitted that it was indeed a likeness of him, but only of his outward parts.

"Now, Lycomedes," he went on, "do you paint a true portrait of your inward self. The colours you must use are faith, meekness, brotherly love, purity, simplicity, and all the Christian virtues. These colours will paint the likeness of your soul; even now they raise up in you what was cast down, and bring down what was puffed up, they tend your bruises, heal your wounds, tidy your hair, wash your face, purge your bowels, empty your belly and cut off what is beneath it; in a word they will present a portrait of you to our Lord Jesus Christ, undaunted, complete and firm of shape. But *this* portrait that you have had made of me is childish and imperfect—it is a dead likeness of the dead."

Though such a holy man, John was not always absorbed by high thoughts and profound meditations. He sometimes relaxed and enjoyed simple and innocent pleasures, and this was apt to scandalise admirers. On one occasion he was sitting in front of a house when a partridge flew down and perched beside him. John picked her up and was gently stroking her feathers when a man dressed as a hunter passed by. He was astonished at the saint's occupation, and asked disdainfully how he could be taken up with such mean amusements. "What are you carrying in your hands?" asked John; and the hunter replied, "A bow." "Why is your bow not properly strung and stretched?" asked the saint. "Because," answered the other, "if it were always stretched it would grow soft and perish, and when it was wanted it would be unable to shoot with vigour." And John answered, "In the same way, young man, the mind needs to be relaxed, lest by constant tension it should lose its vigour."[1]

Our next story is characterised by the author of the *Acts* himself as "a droll matter". John and his followers were travelling

---

[1] This story of John and the partridge comes from Cassian's *Collations* 24: 21. A different version, not so good, is found in the *Acts of John*.

to Ephesus, and as night fell they were obliged to take shelter in a deserted inn. There was a bare bedstead in one of the rooms, on which his friends spread their cloaks for John to sleep on, while they lay on the floor. John, however, was tormented by bugs which came out of the bedstead. They became more and more aggressive, and towards midnight his disciples heard John address them thus: "O bugs, behave yourselves. I call upon you one and all to leave my bed for this one night and remain quiet in one place, and keep your distance from the servants of God." The friends laughed among themselves, but the whole party presently went to sleep and were not disturbed during the night. The next morning when they woke up they were astonished to see a great number of bugs standing motionless at the door of the house. They called John to see the strange spectacle and when he saw how the insects were standing he said to them: "O bugs, since you have behaved yourselves well in obeying my command, return now to your own place." When he had spoken these words the bugs ran from the door, and hastening to the bed climbed up its legs and disappeared into its joints. Then John said to his companions, "These creatures listened to the voice of a man and obeyed it and trespassed no more; but we, when we hear the voice of God, disobey and are light-minded."

By tradition John lived to a very great age. The manner of his death is told in many different ways, from among which we may choose the following.

After giving communion to his friends and partaking of it himself he walked out of the house, bidding two young men follow him, bringing baskets and shovels. When they reached the tomb of one of the brethren he stopped, and told the young men to dig. He made them dig a very deep trench, and when it was finished to his liking he took off his clothes and laid them at the bottom of it, and standing in his shift only, uttered a long prayer. He ended the prayer with the words "Thou art with me, O Lord Jesu Christ"; and lying down in the trench he said to his companions, "Peace be with you, brethren," and gave up his spirit rejoicing.

Did Saint John really die? When his followers returned the following day they could not find his body, but only his sandals and the earth above moving up and down. In St. Augustine's day the belief continued that the earth over the grave was seen to rise and fall as if moved by John's breathing.[1]

Before leaving John we will give two other tales about him which do not come from the *Acts*. The first is told by Irenaeus in his book *Against Heresies*. It was a story, he says, current in the churches of Asia, and reported by Polycarp himself. John, going to the baths of Ephesus, perceived that a certain Cerinthus was within. Thereupon he rushed out of the bath house without bathing, exclaiming, "Let us fly, lest even the bath house fall on our heads, because Cerinthus, the enemy of the truth, is within." The heresy of Cerinthus is described by Irenaeus. He taught that Jesus was born in the ordinary way and was an ordinary man, though more righteous and wise than others. Christ descended on him in the form of a dove at the time of his baptism, but at last departed from him and that then Jesus suffered, while Christ remained without feeling, for he was a spiritual being. It is interesting that something very like this is said in the Apocryphal book to have been the teaching of John himself.

Our other tale comes from a sermon on riches, preached by Clement of Alexandria, who describes it as a true story, handed down in tradition.

When after Domitian's death John was released from Patmos, he went to Ephesus, of which he became the bishop.[2] He used to travel round the countryside, supervising the different churches. In one of them he selected a young man of a pleasing and striking appearance, whom he entrusted to the care of the local presbyter, calling on the members of the Church and Christ

---

[1] Aug. on John 21. *V*. Jesus and Abgar, p. 77.
[2] Domitian died in 96. This story therefore is consistent with the tradition that John lived to a very great age.

Himself to be his witnesses. The presbyter undertook the charge and John returned to Ephesus. The presbyter then took the young man into his house, taught him, cherished him, and finally baptised him; then, thinking the seal of baptism would safeguard him, he relaxed his care and guardianship. Alas! the youth had been emancipated too soon. He fell into bad company, making friends with a party of riotous and dissolute fellows, who completely corrupted him. Costly banquets were followed by nocturnal robberies and the young man was soon leading a life of crime. His energetic and ambitious nature quickly caused him to take the lead and he organised a band of brigands, violent and bloodthirsty, of which he made himself the chief.

Time passed, and John returned to the village where he had left the youth. When he had settled the necessary ecclesiastical business, he said to the presbyter, "Now, pray return me the deposit which, as witnessed by the Church and Christ, I left with you when I was here last." The presbyter at first thought he was being accused of some monetary fraud, and eagerly protested his innocence; but when John explained, "It is the youth I left in your charge, whose soul I now demand back," the old man groaned deeply, and burst into tears. "The man is dead," he said at last. "When and how did he die?" asked John. "He is dead to God," replied the presbyter, "for he turned out utterly depraved, and has taken to the hills, where he is the leader of a robber band." The apostle rent his clothes and beat his head. "I left him in the care of a fine guardian of souls!" he cried. "But bring me at once a horse and a man to guide me to the hills." Without a moment's delay he rode straight from the church door to the hill-country, where he was captured by the robbers' sentry. He did not attempt to escape, but told the sentry to take him to his leader, saying he had come for that very purpose. When he was brought near enough to be recognised the young man, overcome with shame, turned to fly. In spite of his age

John pursued him, crying out, "Why do you fly me, my child, why do you fly your father, an old, unarmed man? Do not be afraid. I will stand surety with Christ for your life—if need be I will give my life for yours. Stop; believe; Christ has sent me." The youth at last stood still, fixing his eyes on the ground. Then he threw down his weapons, and burst into tears. When John came near the robber embraced him, groaning, and held behind his back the right hand that had committed so many crimes. But the apostle solemnly assured him he had won pardon for him from the Saviour. He knelt down, praying and kissing his right hand, purified by repentance, and then led him back to the church. Nor did he leave him till he had restored him to a holy life, and even, it is said, placed him in charge of the church he had at first betrayed.

The Acts of Paul

The *Acts of Paul* is a long, composite book, longer than the canonical *Acts of the Apostles*. A great number of versions in different languages were made; it comprises several sections, probably by different authors, and includes an apocryphal correspondence between Paul and the Corinthians, the episode of Paul and Thecla, and the martyrdom of Paul. We shall deal only with the story of Paul and Thecla. It was immensely popular, and is extant in full in Greek, Latin, Syriac and Coptic. It seems probable that originally it was a separate work, and later was inserted, more or less as a supplement, into the *Acts of Paul*. The story it tells, full of romance and curious details, is worth reading for its own sake; afterwards we shall attempt to analyse it, and thus arrive at the possibility of suggesting the date at which it, or at least part of it, was written.

During the course of Paul's first missionary journey he and his companion Barnabas were obliged by the hostility of the Jews to fly from Antioch and take refuge in Iconium.[1] It is at

[1] Acts 13 and 14.

this moment that our story begins. But the narrator makes no mention of the hostility of the Jews, nor of Barnabas, but says he was accompanied by two false followers, Demas and Hermogenes. There was living in Iconium a certain Onesiphorus, already a Christian, who had heard a description of Paul from another disciple, Titus. He therefore set out towards the royal road which goes to Lystra, to welcome him, and presently saw approaching a man, short of stature, with bow legs, scanty hair, his eyebrows joined together and a long, hooked nose; sometimes he looked like an ordinary man, and sometimes like an angel. Onesiphorus, recognising Paul from the description he had received, embraced him and invited him to stay with him while in Iconium. Paul and his companions accepted the invitation, and on entering the house found an assembly of Christians with whom he prayed and broke bread: he then began to preach on chastity and the resurrection.

The house next door was occupied by a wealthy woman called Theocleia. She had a beautiful daughter, Thecla, who was betrothed to a young man of Iconium named Thamyris. Thecla, seated at her window, listened with rapture to Paul's discourse on chastity; but she could not see him, and envied the women who were clustered round him. For three days and three nights she sat at the window absorbed in listening to the Apostle, and her mother tried in vain to drag her away. At last, in great distress, Theocleia sent for Thamyris, and told him of her daughter's disturbing behaviour. "She hangs on the stranger's words," she said, "like a spider on a thread. Go and speak to her, and try to get her away."

Thamyris spoke to Thecla gently and affectionately, imploring her to come away; but neither the prayers of her betrothed, nor the protestations of her mother, nor the tears of the maid servants, had the least effect. Thecla remained as if in an ecstasy, fascinated by what Paul was saying. At last Thamyris lost all patience. He rushed out into the street, and seeing two men, Demas and Hermogenes, coming out of the neighbouring house, he asked them what was going on, and who the stranger was. The traitors told him they did not know the man, but he was preaching chastity to the maidens and wives of the city. They advised him to lodge a complaint with the governor of the city, who would doubtless put an end to the man's preaching and restore his betrothed to Thamyris.

Thamyris took their advice. He went with a posse of soldiers to the house of Onesiphorus, dragged Paul out, haled him before the governor, and accused him of corrupting the women of the town. The governor questioned Paul, and after hearing his defence—that he was teaching the word of God—detained him in prison while considering what course of action to pursue.

When night fell Thecla took action. The door of her mother's house was shut up, but she bribed the porter with her bracelets and persuaded him to let her out. She then made her way to the prison where Paul was confined, and by the gift of her silver mirror induced the jailor to admit her. For the rest of the night she sat at Paul's feet, kissing his chains and listening to his wonderful words.

The next morning Theocleia was horrified to find that Thecla was not in the house. After some enquiry the door-keeper confessed that he had let her out, and that she had gone to the prison where Paul lay. The matter was reported to the governor, who sent for them both. He questioned Thecla as to why she now refused to marry Thamyris, but she made no answer, keeping her eyes fixed on the Apostle. Theocleia, beyond herself with rage, called out, "Burn the rebellious girl! Burn her in the arena, as a warning to others who may have been led away by this sorcerer!" The governor, much disturbed by these occurrences, gave orders that Paul was to be scourged and expelled from the city, and Thecla burnt as her mother had suggested.

When Thecla was brought into the arena she looked everywhere in the crowd for Paul. She thought she saw him sitting among the people; but it was in reality the Lord himself, who had taken on the likeness of Paul; and as she gazed fixedly at him he ascended into heaven and disappeared. She was placed naked on the pyre, which was then lighted; but the fire did not take hold of her. A noise of thunder was heard, and a terrific storm broke out, overwhelming the spectators with rain and hail. They fled in all directions, and in the confusion Thecla made her escape.

Meanwhile Paul, Onesiphorus and his household had left the city and taken refuge in an open sepulchre by the roadside. They remained there for some days until their food was exhausted, when Paul sent one of the boys back to Iconium to buy some bread. This boy came across Thecla, who was wandering about, searching for Paul, and at her request he led her to the place where the Apostle was hiding. All the company rejoiced at Thecla's escape from the flames, and she cried out eagerly, "I will cut off my hair and follow you, Paul, wherever you go." "You are too beautiful," replied Paul, "you might fall into temptation and danger." "Baptise me," she answered, "and I shall be safe." But Paul told her to have patience—she should be baptised later. He then bade Onesiphorus and his family return to Iconium, and taking Thecla by the hand went with her to Antioch.

At Antioch a great festival was in progress. A rich and prominent citizen, one Alexander, was giving a show of wild beasts in the amphitheatre—a show of an official and religious character. Alexander, in his ceremonial clothes—a mantle and a crown bearing the image of Caesar—was on his way to the amphitheatre, when he met Paul and Thecla entering the city. At the first glance Alexander was overwhelmed by the beauty of the girl, and was seized by a passionate love for her. Seeing her alone in the company of a man he naturally assumed she was his slave, and immediately offered Paul a large sum of money if he would hand her over to him. "I do not know the woman," said Paul. "She does not belong to me." Paul's behaviour in this matter is decidedly peculiar, but there is no explanation of it. Alexander, seeing she was without a protector, must have supposed she was a woman of easy virtue—for who else would be alone in the streets? He therefore flung his arms round her and embraced her. Thecla cried out, in great agitation, "I am of noble birth, I come from Iconium, I am a servant of God." She claimed, in fact, the rights of a guest, a stranger and a religious devotee. Alexander, however, inflamed by passion, paid no attention to her protest and persisted in his embraces. Thereupon Thecla tore his mantle, snatched off his crown, bearing the image of the Emperor, and flung it on the ground.

By this action Thecla had become guilty both of high treason and sacrilege, for the person of an official in Alexander's position was sacrosanct. His feelings can easily be imagined. His advances had been repulsed, he had been insulted and publicly humiliated, and his love turned to fury. He brought Thecla before the proconsul, and, when she admitted what she had done, managed that she should be condemned to be thrown to the wild beasts on the following day. The women of the town, accepting Thecla's story that she was the votary of a god, were outraged at this decision, and called out, "A wicked judgement! An impious judgement!" On hearing this cry Thecla took heart, and begged the proconsul to allow her to spend the night before her punishment in the house of a woman, that her virtue might be protected. This was granted her, and she was handed over to the care of Tryphaena, who, we are told, was "a rich queen", "a kinswoman of Caesar". While the procession in honour of the games was passing through the streets, Thecla was placed on a cage containing a lioness, and set in the arena. On the cage was a placard with the word *Sacrilega*—guilty of sacrilege. It was observed with amazement that the lioness put her tongue between the bars of the cage and licked Thecla's bare feet. After the procession Thecla was taken down and handed over to Tryphaena.

Now Tryphaena was a queen and a widow, whose daughter, Falconilla, had recently died. She had appeared to her mother in a dream and said to her, "Mother, take in my place Thecla, the stranger who is desolate in our city; she will pray for me, that I may enter into the place of righteousness." So when Tryphaena had received Thecla into her house she told her of her vision, and Thecla immediately prayed to God that Falconilla should be saved. And Tryphaena loved Thecla like a second child, and deeply grieved for her terrible fate.

At daybreak next day Alexander arrived to take Thecla away, but Tryphaena made great lamentation, saying, "I am bereft of my daughter a second time, and there is no one to help me, for I am a widow." Alexander therefore left the house, and presently the soldiers came for their prisoner and took her away, Tryphaena holding her hand and accompanying her to the place where she was to suffer.

The amphitheatre was packed with spectators, some crying "Bring in the sacrilegious woman!" others, especially the women, calling out, "An impious judgement has fallen on the city." Thecla was placed in the arena and a fierce lioness was loosed upon her. But to the amazement of all, the lioness only lay down and licked her feet.[1] Then a leopard was let out, but when he was about to leap on the girl the lioness fell upon him and tore him to pieces. A bear next came out, but the lioness killed him too. Then a terrible lion rushed at her. The lioness fought him like the rest, and in the combat both beasts perished. Meanwhile, Thecla stood in the arena praying. And suddenly she noticed a great tank of water in which many fierce seals were swimming. She exclaimed, "Now it is time for my baptism," and she ran towards it and jumped in, crying out, "In the name of Jesus Christ I baptise myself, before I die." At that moment there was a flash of lightning which killed the seals, and their dead bodies floated to the top of the tank. More wild beasts were now sent out upon her,

[1] Cf. the story of Androcles and the Lion.

but the women in the audience shrieked aloud, and threw in scented leaves, incense and other perfumes so that the wild beasts were stupefied and lay down as if asleep. Alexander went to the judge and said, "I have two wild bulls. We will tie her to them and they will tear her apart." "Do as you like," replied the judge. Thecla's feet were attached to the bulls with ropes, and the animals were stirred up by red-hot irons; but when the frightened bulls leaped forward the fire burnt the ropes and Thecla was released.

When Tryphaena, who was present at this horrible scene, saw Thecla tied to the bulls, she gave a loud cry and fainted. All the people, thinking she was dead, were in great consternation. The governor stopped the games, and Alexander himself was alarmed. He fell at the governor's feet, crying out, "Let the woman go; for if Caesar hears of his kinswoman's death he will destroy the city and all of us who are in it." So the governor agreed to release her, saying to the people, "A god has delivered Thecla." And all the people cried out, "The god who delivered Thecla is a great god"; and the whole city shook with the sound of their acclamation.

When Tryphaena had recovered her senses she embraced Thecla, saying, "Now I believe in the resurrection; now I believe that my daughter still lives. Come with me. I will make you heir of all I possess." So Thecla went with her and stayed in her house for eight days, teaching her and all her household.

But Thecla longed to be with Paul again. She sent messengers to look for him, far and wide, and at last found he was in a town called Myra. She cut off her hair, dressed as a man, and accompanied by a party of servants set off to join him. She found him preaching in the market-place. But when he saw her surrounded by men he was amazed, and wondered whether she had fallen into temptation. Thecla saw what he suspected, and reassured him, telling him she had received baptism. So Paul took her into the house of Hermias where he was staying and heard all her story. All who were present glorified God, and prayed for the good queen Tryphaena. Then Thecla departed for her own home in Iconium, leaving with Paul the gold and rich clothing that Tryphaena had given her, that he might distribute them among the poor. When she arrived at Iconium she found that Thamyris was dead. She tried to convert her mother; some say she succeeded, others that she failed. In any case she eventually went to Seleucia, where she lived to the age of ninety, and died, in the odour of sanctity.

When was this little romance written? For a long time it was dated towards A.D. 160. Tertullian, who towards the end of his life became a Montanist, and supporter of women preachers,[1] was in his earlier days an orthodox believer and opponent of the ministry of women. In one of his writings— belonging to his pre-heretical time—he makes an attack on the *Acts of Paul*, presumably for its feminist tendencies. It was, he declares, the work of a presbyter of Asia, who confessed he had concocted it for the love of Paul, and who was in conse- quence ejected from the priesthood. This seemed to show the book was composed in the second half of the second century, and for a long time this date was accepted. In the beginning of the twentieth century, however, the question was raised anew. The book was carefully analysed, and it became probable that it had been continually revised and interpolated. It is impos- sible to go into all the details here;[2] the most interesting ques- tion is at what date we may place its original form.

It will be remembered that Onesiphorus went out to meet Paul "going towards the Royal Road which goes to Lystra," that is, he walked along a side road from Iconium until he reached the point at which it met the main road between Antioch and Lystra. Sir William Ramsay, an expert in the topography of Asia Minor, has pointed out that the road

[1] *V.* A Vanished Sect, p. 168.
[2] *V.* Ramsay. *Church in the Roman Empire before A.D.* 170.

between Antioch and Lystra ceased to be a main road towards A.D. 74, when Lystra declined in importance, its place being taken by Iconium. After that time the main road from Antioch went to Iconium, and it would be unnatural to say that a man walked from Iconium "until he came to the Royal Road leading to Lystra". A mere detail, of course, but a

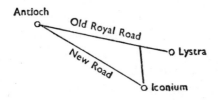

most significant one. Is it probable or even possible that anyone writing in the second century should have remembered the old road, or that he should have troubled to insert such an allusion to it in his text? It seems certain that this passage at least must have been written before the end of the first century, and by someone who was personally acquainted with the district at that date.

Even more significant is the figure of Queen Tryphaena. Who was this queen, who plays such an important part in the story of Thecla? For a long time she was quite unknown to history—she is not mentioned by any classical historian. But since 1902 her figure has emerged from the shadows, and thanks to many inscriptions, coins and medals, her biography has been recovered and may be found in an account of her by Mommsen.[1]

Antonia Tryphaena was a cousin of the Emperor Claudius— she was, as the *Acts* tells us, a kinswoman of Caesar. She married Cotys, King of Thrace, who left her a widow in A.D. 19. Her three sons became kings of Thrace and Pontus, but in A.D. 48 she quarrelled with them and retired to her

[1] *Ephemeris Epigraphica.*

private estates. It will be remembered that she cries out, "There is no one to help me, for I am a widow," but the governor of Antioch fears the Emperor's wrath if any harm should befall her. In A.D. 54 Claudius died and was succeeded by Nero, who was no relation to her and would probably not have extended any favour towards her. The story therefore may be placed between the years 48 and 54. Just as the topography of the roads must have been speedily forgotten, so was the Queen Tryphaena. Could such correct details possibly have been supplied a hundred years later? It may also be pointed out that though the exact dates of Paul's biography are uncertain, his visit to Iconium is placed by most students between A.D. 47 and 51, and the author of the book was, it would seem, a very near contemporary of his, and a dweller in the locality he writes about. What then are we to think of his description of Paul's appearance? He was "short of stature, with bow legs, scanty hair and a long hooked nose". Not an idealised portrait of a saint, surely, but a vivid picture by an eyewitness, of a living man. And the presbyter who said he wrote "for the love of Paul" did not write, we may conjecture, for love of his fame, but for love of the great Apostle himself.

The Assumption of the Virgin

All the apocryphal writings we have been considering so far belong to the second century. Those dealing with the Assumption of the Virgin are much later. James says, "I cannot regard any of them as older than the fourth century, but the nucleus of the story may be—I think must be—at least as old as the third."[1] He adds that he believes the legend was first elaborated, if it did not originate, in Egypt. In any case there are extant a great number of texts in different languages—a Greek writing, attributed to St. John, one in Latin attributed to Joseph of Arimathea, besides those in Coptic, Aramaic, Syriac, Arabic

[1] *Apocryphal New Testament* p. xix.

and Ethiopic. There is great variety in their accounts of the Virgin's death—not all of them speak of bodily assumption, and only one, the Latin version attributed to Joseph of Arimathea, gives the episode of Thomas and the girdle. Though divergent throughout from most of the other narratives, it seems to be the one that had the greatest influence on medieval thought. The story runs as follows:

In the second year after the Ascension, Mary was in her house praying, when the angel Gabriel appeared before her, bearing a palm; he announced that she was to die three days later, and presented her with the palm.

By this time the Apostles were dispersed and were preaching in different parts of the world. Mary summoned Joseph of Arimathea and the other disciples and told them of her approaching death; there followed an earthquake and a violent storm of thunder and rain in the midst of which all the apostles except Thomas were brought on clouds, and descended at the door of her house. She told them, too, that she was about to die, and all the company prepared for the event, praying and singing hymns throughout the night. The next day was the Sabbath, and early in the morning Christ, surrounded by a crowd of angels, descended from the sky and took the soul of Mary. As he ascended with it to heaven there was another earthquake and all Jerusalem, in a flash, saw that Mary was dead. The Jews, who had become possessed by Satan, determined to burn the body and kill the apostles, but before they could execute their purpose they were struck by blindness and rushed impotently to and fro, striking their heads against walls and hitting each other with their sticks.

The apostles lifted up the body and carried it to the valley of Jehoshaphat[1] where they intended to bury it. On the way they were intercepted by a Jew named Reuben, who tried to upset the bier; but when he touched it his arms withered and

---

[1] A valley along the east side of Jerusalem.

his hands stuck immovably to the bier, so that he was obliged to follow the funeral procession. Weeping and groaning, he implored the apostles to release him. At their prayer his hands were unloosed, whereupon he declared his belief in Christ, and at his urgent request the apostles baptised him.

They then continued on their way and, reaching the burial place, placed the body reverently in the tomb, weeping and singing hymns. All at once a bright light shone around them, and they fell to earth and saw nothing. At the same time, Thomas, who had been saying mass in India, was suddenly transported to the spot, still wearing his priestly vestments. He gazed at the tomb, and alone of all the apostles saw the body of Mary taken up into heaven by the holy angels. He cried out to her as she rose, "Thou art going to heaven. Have mercy on thy servant and make him rejoice"; and thereupon the girdle, with which the apostles had bound the body, was thrown down to him and he caught it in his hands. When he joined the other apostles, who were quite unaware of what had happened, they jeered at him, and told him that because he had not believed in the Lord's resurrection he had been found unworthy to be present at the burial of his mother. Thomas meekly admitted his sin, and asked where they had buried her. They pointed to the tomb, whereupon he said, "The body is not there." Peter indignantly rebuked him as an unbeliever, and when he reiterated that the body was not there they turned angrily from him and lifted up the stone that covered the tomb. Just as Thomas had said, the tomb was empty, and the apostles were struck dumb with amazement. Thomas then told them that he had witnessed the ascension of Mary and that she had thrown him the girdle which he showed them. The apostles, quite confounded, asked his pardon, and he blessed them, and said, "Behold how good and pleasant a thing it is, brethren, to live together in unity."[1]

In some accounts Mary's death is announced to her by Jesus

[1] The Virgin's girdle is now the great relic in the Cathedral of Prato.

himself. She is frightened, but Jesus comforts her and promises to protect her. At the moment of death her soul leaps out of her body and Jesus receives it in his bosom. In some accounts the Assumption does not take place till a considerable time—seven months—two hundred and six days—after the burial. Jesus appears in a chariot carried by the Cherubim, bearing his mother's soul. The coffin, which had been shut like Noah's ark, opens, the body rises and embraces its own soul—"they are like two brothers who are come from a strange country and are united one with another". Two Coptic versions mention a great voice which says, "Let no man trouble to seek for the body, till the great day of the returning of Christ." This is rather mysterious. It seems to imply that the body, though not to be found, is actually in the earth; but it may well have suggested the story of the Assumption to later writers.

In any case it is interesting to find that one of these narratives (which one?) so long thought to be apocryphal, is after all true. In 1950 the Pope revealed that the Assumption of the Virgin's body actually took place, and this is now *de fide* for all Catholics. The only other mortals who are in heaven, intact with their bodies, are Enoch and Elijah, who, like her, as we may read in the Old Testament, were taken up bodily into heaven.

VI

Theologians

THE Church has always had to combat two classes of enemy—the undisguised heathen wolves, and the more dangerous heretical teachers who in Christian clothing entered the fold and ravaged the flock from within. During the second century the most menacing of these insidious enemies of the truth were the Gnostics, whose wild and sinister doctrines were a perpetual threat to orthodox religion.

Gnosticism had existed long before Christianity and was prevalent in the East and especially in Egypt in many varying forms. It was in principle an attempt to reconcile the idea of an abstract and ineffable God with a concrete and material world. The Gnostics achieved a link between the two apparently incompatible conceptions in two ways—first by the mystical experience of a direct communion with God, and second by an occult lore of secret rites, watchwords, names and numbers. In these ways they acquired their Gnosis or Knowledge, and hence were called Gnostics—those who knew. With the rise of Christianity there came a fusion of the two beliefs—many Gnostics became Christians, many Christians became Gnostics, and an enormous number of sects appeared, varying in their outlook and way of life, each claiming to be the true exponents of Gnosis.

Irenaeus and the Gnostics

It was to save Christianity from these erroneous teachings that Irenaeus (c. 120–202) wrote his great book *Against Heresies*. In it he expounds and controverts more than twenty Gnostic sects, which, varied as they are, have for the most part certain ideas in common. Matter, being evil, could not emanate from God, and the world was created by angels, or inferior spirits, one of whom, named the Demiurge or Work-man, is often said to be the Creator spoken of in the Old Testament. Marcion, one of the most eminent of these here-tics, taught that the creator of the Old Testament was the author of all evils, who delighted in war and was infirm of purpose and self-contradictory. Those who disobeyed him were faithful to the Supreme God and therefore were the true righteous. Hence Christ, on his descent into Hell, drew out Cain, the Sodomites, the Egyptians and all the heathen. Abel, Noah, Abraham and the other patriarchs thought that God was merely tempting them as he so often did. They refused to believe Christ's teaching, and consequently remained behind in Hell. As the body is material it is evil, and will not take part in the Resurrection. Their teaching as regards Jesus was Docetic—that is to say he only appeared to have a body. He passed through Mary, Valentinus taught, as water flows through a pipe. The Spirit, they said, descended on him in the shape of a dove at his baptism, or at the marriage at Cana, where he performed his first miracle. It was only a phantom body that suffered crucifixion. Basilides tells us that Simon of Cyrene, who carried his cross, was magically transformed into the figure of Jesus and crucified in his stead, while Jesus himself received the form of Simon and standing by laughed at them. Or if his body was indeed crucified, at that very moment his divinity left him, which explains the cry from the cross "My God, my God, why hast thou forsaken me?"

Many of the Gnostics were sorcerers. Simon Magus[1] was, as his name implies, a great magician, who thought the Apostles performed their cures by the use of magic.[2] He offered them money, if they would reveal their secret to him, and from this comes the word *simony*, meaning the buying or selling of ecclesiastical preferment. His followers used exorcisms and incantations, and pressed into their service love-potions and charms, as well as familiar spirits and dream

[1] *V*. p. 78, et seq.   [2] Acts 8: 9-12.

makers. Another Gnostic magician was a certain Marcus, who performed conjuring tricks at a form of the Eucharist, in which he filled a large cup from a small one which he caused his women devotees to consecrate. He made many women disciples, especially those who were well-bred, elegantly dressed and very wealthy, but he did not neglect those of a humbler position. He went to stay with a deacon who had a wife of remarkable beauty. Marcus corrupted her both body and soul, and for a long time travelled about with her. At last she was rescued by the brethren, and recognising the error of her ways spent the rest of her life making public confession of her sins and lamenting the defilement she had suffered from the magician. All these heretics made use of magic words and numbers; some had secret marks on their bodies, branding the inside of the lobe of the right ear. They had many crowned and painted images, among them a likeness of Christ which they said was made by Pontius Pilate.[1] These secret marks, names and numbers formed part of the Gnostic system of redemption. Man, they taught, was controlled by certain wicked guardian demons. To win freedom the soul must ascend through various spheres, deceiving or subduing the demons by charms and passwords. If it succeeded in escaping the demons the soul would return to its original home in the heavenly light and be reunited with the celestial beings who dwell there. Redemption is, however, only for a limited number. Material natures cannot be saved, and spiritual natures will certainly be saved, animal natures, between the material and spiritual, may be saved by good works.[2]

Many of the Gnostics were, however, antinomians—that is, they did not hold themselves obliged to obey any moral law, but would attain salvation whatever their actions in this life— every kind of criminal behaviour was a matter of perfect indifference. Some of them, however, held a very different

[1] *V.* Jesus and Abgar, p. 70.
[2] This certainly seems to resemble some Christian teaching.

doctrine. They were severely ascetic, forbade any carnal relations, and would not baptise married people unless they broke off all intercourse. Many refused all animal food and would not touch wine—even the sacrament of the Eucharist was pure water. Some Gnostic sects also taught the transmigration of souls. Further they explained the objection that their teaching differed manifestly from that of the Gospel by declaring that Jesus gave his true teaching secretly—his disciples were only to impart it to those who were worthy.

There was a vast Gnostic literature most of which, like other heretical writings, has disappeared—probably deliberately destroyed by the orthodox. But besides the philosophical writings of the learned, religious-minded Gnostics, we find among the Apocryphal writings, already discussed in the previous section, a number of more popular books tainted with Gnostic or at least docetic doctrine.

The first part of Irenaeus's work *Against Heresies* is devoted to expounding the curious doctrines of the Gnostics. In the rest of his book he refutes them, chiefly by quoting the Bible, both the Old and New Testaments. Into this refutation it is not necessary for us to enter, as his argument is in the main purely theological. There are, however, two curious points which it is worth while to mention. It will be remembered that he rebukes the heretics for the use they make of the mystical importance of numbers. He himself is, however, not immune to the idea.

"It is not possible," he says, "that the Gospels can be more or less in number than they are. For there are four zones of the world and four principal winds . . . and the cherubim too were four-faced." He goes on to quote the Book of Revelation, which tells us that the first of these faces was a lion, the second a calf, the third a man and the fourth an eagle. We all know that these figures are traditionally associated with the Evangelists, and have influenced Christian art from early times. The Fathers agreed as to the general interpretation of the symbols, but differed widely as to the details. St. Jerome's scheme was accepted in the West. The Man represents Matthew, the Lion Mark, the Ox Luke, and the Eagle John. John was the greatest of the Evangelists and the lectern which supports the Bible in our churches is usually in the form of an eagle.

One other noteworthy idea of Irenaeus must be recounted. The Lord, he says, passed through and sanctified every age; he was an infant, a child, a youth, that infants, children and young men should be given an example of virtue, and that each age should be sanctified. "So likewise," he continues, "he was an old man for old men." He justifies this surprising statement by pointing out that John's Gospel clearly indicates the truth. "Thou art not yet fifty years old and hast thou seen Abraham?" the Jews asked him (John 8:57). "They mentioned a period near his real age (i.e. 48 or 49), whether they had ascertained this out of the entry in the public register or simply made a conjecture from what they observed." Irenaeus adds, "The elders . . . who were conversant in Asia with John the disciple of the Lord, affirm that John told them so. Some of the elders, moreover, saw not only John but the other apostles also and heard the very same account from them."

This curious tradition has not left many traces. We may, however, mention that an apocryphal writing, *The Acts of Pilate* (date quite uncertain), claims in some versions to be an official report on the trial and execution of Christ sent to the Emperor Claudius. As Claudius became Emperor in A.D. 41 the crucifixion must have taken place when Christ was in his forties. Some modern writers, who think that John's Gospel must be taken throughout symbolically, see in the passage a suggestion that the Lord had reached the mystic age of forty-nine.

The Story of Narcissus

Narcissus, bishop of Jerusalem, was a remarkable and holy man. His story is told by Eusebius in his Ecclesiastical History.

He became bishop about A.D. 180 at the age of eighty-four; he was therefore born in A.D. 96, and was a survivor of the Apostolic Age. Curiously enough we know nothing about him before he was consecrated bishop; his recorded history is concerned only with the years of his episcopate and his old age.

The Church of Jerusalem was in origin Jewish; that is to say its members, though believing that Christ was the promised Messiah, still held to the Jewish Law, from which St. Paul and his followers broke away. But after Hadrian took Jerusalem and expelled the Jews the Church fell into the hands of the orthodox Christians and the Jewish Christians soon disappeared. Narcissus, we are told, was the fifteenth bishop of the non-Jewish community. In A.D. 195 at the age of 99 he presided with Theophilus of Caesarea at the Synod of Palestine. This Synod condemned the Eastern practice of observing the day of the Lord's death on the 14th of Nisan, the date of the Jewish Passover, and adopted the Western custom fixing the date of Easter so that it always fell on a Sunday.

It may well be that the decision of the Synod for which Narcissus was perhaps held responsible roused ill-feeling among the adherents of the old custom. At all events his enemies attempted to bring about his downfall.

"Certain miserable creatures," says Eusebius, "not being able to endure his energy and the firmness of his conduct, and fearing lest they should be taken and put on their trial (for they were conscious of many evil deeds) anticipated the event by devising an intrigue against him, and spreading a certain grave slander to his hurt." These villains supported their accusations by calling down imprecations on their own heads if they spoke falsely. "If this is not true," said one, "may I be destroyed by fire"; "May I fall into a fatal disease," said the second; and the third, "May I become blind." Though none of the faithful were taken in, Narcissus was so much distressed by these slanderous tales he fled from Jerusalem and hid himself in some unknown part of the adjacent desert. It was not long before God took the three perjurers at their word. The first was burnt to death with all his family, a small spark having accidentally set fire to his house. The second "was covered from head to foot with the disease he had assigned to himself as a penalty". The third, horrified at the judgement that had overtaken his two accomplices, publicly confessed his crimes, and wept so profusely in his repentance that he lost the sight of both his eyes.

Narcissus was now vindicated. But as he had disappeared and no one knew where to find him, his flock decided to choose another bishop. Dius, who was first appointed, was followed by Germanion, Germanion by Gordius. In his day Narcissus unexpectedly reappeared and was acclaimed by the brethren, who without delay reinstated him in the bishopric.

By this time, however, Narcissus was, it seems, too old to manage the affairs of the church, and the brethren decided to give him a coadjutor. Who was this to be? The most zealous of them received a revelation during the night, bidding them go outside the gates of the city and welcome as their bishop the man who should come to them. The man they saw was Alexander, a bishop of Cappadocia, who, it so happened, had been instructed by a vision to visit Jerusalem. It was thus clear that Alexander was fore-ordained to be co-bishop of Jerusalem. He was seized by the zealous brethren and compelled to remain with them. Alexander, in a letter to an Egyptian community of Christians, wrote "in these very words, at the close of the letter: 'Narcissus greets you, who before me was bishop here, and now is associated with me in the prayers, having completed 116 years'." This letter, says Eusebius, "is still to this day preserved with us".

Eusebius has another story of this long-lived bishop, though he gives no indication of the moment in his career at which the episode took place. One year, at the vigil before Easter, the deacons, whose business it was to light the lamps, discovered that they had run short of oil. The congregation was plunged in despondency and gloom; but Narcissus was equal to the occasion. He ordered the deacons to draw water and bring it to him. He prayed over it, and the water, when poured into the lamps, proved to have been miraculously changed into oil. This marvellous oil lasted a long time, and some of it was preserved to the days of Eusebius himself, thus proving the great powers of Narcissus. This story—the tradition of Jerusalem—as Cardinal Newman points out, "had but a narrow interval to pass from Narcissus to Eusebius—not above fifty or sixty years". "On the whole, then," he adds, "there seems sufficient ground to justify us in accepting this narrative."

Clement of Alexandria

Clement of Alexandria was born about A.D. 150, and died about 210. He was one of the most learned of the early Fathers and spent the greater part of his life in Alexandria. Alexandria had been for many years a cultural centre of the highest importance. It had two great libraries, and students gathered there to study literature and especially science—among its alumni we hear of Euclid (450–380 B.C.) and Galen (c. A.D. 200). In fact it was what we should nowadays call a university town. It was also important commercially—the most important market-port of the Roman world, and many of its inhabitants were wealthy and luxurious merchants. Alexandria was also a religious centre. Worshippers of every creed were to be found there. The pagan deities, the Roman Emperors, the local native cults, all had their shrines there. The Jews had their own quarter with many synagogues, and even as early as A.D. 200 there was a Christian group and a school for Christian students. We do not know much about the early history of this school—but it seems to have had no separate building; the teachers gave instruction in their own houses. There would doubtless be different classes for the recently converted and for the more advanced among the faithful, and it was in teaching these classes that Clement was engaged during his twenty years in the city.

Clement's extant works consist of a sermon—*What Rich Man is being saved?*[1] and three longer treatises: *The Prolepticon* or *Exhortation to the Heathen, The Pedagogue* and *Stromateis,* variously rendered *Bundles, Patchwork, Clothesbags* or more prosaically *Miscellanies.* These three books deal with different stages in the Christian life. *The Prolepticon* is in the nature of an Apology, and is for the use of those who are hovering on the verge of conversion. *The Pedagogue* is a book of practical instruction to those who have recently become Christians, while *Stromateis,* as its name suggests, is a collection of miscellaneous speculations addressed to advanced believers, and deals with philosophical and theological matters in such a way as to lead them to the higher knowledge or Christian gnosis.

1. THE PROLEPTICON. From this book we shall give a few selections, to give some idea of Clement's method of dealing with his subject.

Eunomos and the Grasshopper. The Greeks had met together at Delphi to celebrate the death of the Pythic serpent, and were applauding Eunomos the Locrian, who was singing of the reptile's death. Whether it was a hymn of triumph or a dirge I cannot say, but there was a musical contest, and Eunomos was accompanying himself on the lyre. It was a burning hot day and the grasshoppers were singing on the hills, hidden by the leaves . . . not, of course, for the dead dragon, but for the all-wise God—and they sang according to their own rules, much superior to the rules of Eunomos. The Locrian breaks a string of his lyre. The grasshopper springs on to the neck of the instrument, and sings as if on the branch of a tree, and the player, adapting his song to that of the grasshopper, thus made up for the loss of a string.

The Muses. The Muses, whom Alcander calls the daughters of Zeus and Mnemosyne, and whom other poets and writers

[1] *V.* p. III.

consider and venerate as goddesses, in whose honour whole cities have erected Museums, were in reality maid-servants. They were bought by Megaclo, the daughter of Makar. This Makar, King of the Lesbians, was always on bad terms with his wife, and Megaclo was vexed for her mother's sake. What could she do to improve matters? She bought the Mysian servants, how many is not known, and called them Mysae, in the Aeolian dialect. She taught them to sing the deeds of men of old, accompanying themselves on the lyre. Their beautiful music soothed Makar, and put an end to his bad temper. So Megaclo, in gratitude to them for her mother's sake, had bronze statues made of them, and ordered them to be honoured in all the temples. These then were the Muses.

The Greeks themselves despise their idols. The tyrant Dionysius the Younger removed the golden mantle of the statue of Zeus in Sicily, and ordered him to be dressed in a woollen one. He remarked, humorously, that it would be better than the golden one, as it was lighter in summer and warmer in winter. . . . Phidias the Athenian inscribed on the finger of his Olympian Zeus "Pantarkos is beautiful". It was not Zeus who was beautiful in his eyes, but the boy he loved. . . .[1] Praxiteles, when he made the statue of Aphrodite of Cnidus, carved her in the likeness of Cratine, the girl he loved, so that the wretched people of the city should worship his own mistress. . . . The Romans, who attributed all their success to Fortune, whom they worshipped as a great goddess, installed her statue in a privy, giving over to her a temple they judged worthy of her—a latrine.

The Heathen Gods were really men. "Those whom you worship were once men, and in process of time died; but myths and time have crowned them with honour. People readily come to despise the present because they live in it; whilst the past, which cannot be directly examined and is hidden in the darkness of ages, is invested with honour by imagination and

---

[1] Pantarkos means "all powerful" and might apply to Zeus as well as to the beloved of Phidias.

fiction. We are suspicious of the present, full of admiration for the past. In this way the dead men of antiquity, being reverenced through the long prevalence of error, are thought to be gods by their successors."

Heathen Priests. "Just look at those amongst you who minister to the idols. Their hair is dirty, their clothes are filthy and disgustingly torn; they never go near a bath, their nails are long as the claws of wild beasts, many of them are castrated. All this shows that the temples are in reality nothing but graves or prisons. These men seem to lament the gods rather than to worship them and to be more deserving of pity than piety."

2. THE PEDAGOGUE. When we think of the early Christians we are apt to suppose that they were to be found mostly among the slaves and poorer classes—this was in fact a reproach often levelled against Christianity by its pagan opponents. But in Alexandria there was undoubtedly a considerable section of wealthy persons who belonged to the new religion. The only one of Clement's sermons that has been preserved is entitled *What Rich Man is being saved?*[1], and as we shall see his book on manners is addressed to the prosperous well-to-do who in their heathen days had lived luxuriously and extravagantly, in a way quite unsuitable to their new profession of faith. It was to instruct these converts in the manners suitable to Christians that Clement wrote this book. The Pedagogue, who gives us instructions on morals and manners, is Christ, the Son of God.

Clement begins with the question of eating. "Some men," he says, "live that they may eat, but we should rather eat that we may live." Food should be simple, "ministering to life, not luxury". He is especially shocked by the fact that people take so much trouble to get food from all parts of the world—turbots from Attica, lampreys from Sicily, even beetroot, figs and turnips are brought from all over the Empire. (Here the modern man parts company from Clement. The most devout Christian no longer thinks it wrong to buy butter from New

[1] *V.* Acts of John, p. III.

Zealand or tea from Ceylon.) Not content with these exotic foods, Clement continues, "the gluttons gape for sauces". They surround themselves with hissing frying-pans and wear away their lives at the pestle and mortar. They even go so far as to "emasculate plain food, namely bread, by straining off the nourishing part of the grain." It is interesting to notice that even today most of our bread is still emasculated in this way, though some of it would meet with Clement's approval.

Clement goes on to speak of table manners. "How foolish for people to raise themselves on their couches, all but pitching their faces into the dishes, stretching out from the couch as from a nest; how senseless to smear their hands with the sauces, cramming themselves immoderately and shamelessly. Such people are more like pigs or dogs in their gluttony, in such a hurry to fill themselves that the perspiration runs down their faces. They push the food with disgusting avidity into their stomachs, as if they were stowing their victuals away for provision on a journey."

Such behaviour is not suitable for Christians. "We should abstain from such low-class manners and touch what is set before us in a decorous way, keeping the hand and couch and chin free from stains, committing no impropriety in the act of swallowing, but stretching out the hand at intervals in an orderly manner. We must guard against speaking while we eat, nor is it suitable to eat and drink at the same time." "Take small helpings," he adds, "and do not take too much sauce."

As regards drinking, Clement advocates a moderate use of wine, and quotes the well-known epistle to Timothy, "Use a little wine for thy stomach's sake." But drinking to excess is unhealthy and has most unpleasant consequences: "The lips are relaxed, the eyes roll wildly, the feet are carried from a man as by a flood, and hiccoughing and maudlin nonsense follow." Clement continues with a disgustingly realistic description of a drunken man. The Christian must pay regard to decency, "so that we are to drink without contortions of the face, not greedily grasping the cup. Nor should we drain the cup at a draught, nor besprinkle the chin nor splash the garments as we gulp down the liquor, our face almost filling the bowl and drowned in it".

These gluttonous methods of eating and drinking lead to unpleasant noises—"a gurgling as the drink rushes violently down, while the throat makes a noise, through the rapidity of ingurgitation." All such noises are to be shunned—frequent spitting and violent clearing of the throat—sneezing and hiccoughing should be managed quietly and not emphasised. Many wipe their noses and spit even while supping, scrape their teeth and scratch their ears. Even fidgeting and changing one's position at table is unseemly. "Let the look be steady, and the turning of the neck and motions of the hands in conversation decorous."

"After the bath," says Clement, "having returned thanks to God for having spent a happy day, we must turn our thoughts to sleep. Magnificent bed-clothes, gold-embroidered carpets, long robes of fine purple, costly fleecy cloaks . . . are to be banished." "Moreover silver-footed couches are ostentatious, and ivory beds . . . are not permissible for holy men. . . ." On the other hand it savours of cynic vanity for a man to act as Diomedes—"And he stretched himself under a wild bull's hide"[1]—unless compelled by circumstances.

Feather beds, besides being unduly voluptuous, are bad for the health. The body sinks into a hollow, on either side of which a hill rises, so that it is impossible to turn in them. A flat, even bed enables the sleeper to roll, and this natural gymnastic movement aids the digestion, and "renders them fitter for emergencies". Ulysses and Jacob are commended for using stones for pillows.

Too much food before going to bed is the cause of bad dreams. "The hiccoughing of those who are loaded with wine and the snorting of those who are stuffed with food, and the

[1] Iliad 16: 155.

141

snoring rolled in the bed-clothes and the rumbling of pained stomachs render the eye of the soul blind, by filling the mind with ten thousand phantasies."

Clement has a great deal to say on sleeping too long. "Much sleep is not good for the body or the soul." A man who is asleep might as well be dead. Consequently a good Christian should not sleep right through the night. A woman should get up from time to time and ply her distaff, a man should devote himself to literature or practise his art; but one should not make up for this by sleeping during the day. "Fits of inertia, napping, stretching oneself, yawning, are proofs of frivolous uneasiness of the soul. And it must be observed that the soul never sleeps—it is ceaselessly active; and when it is distracted from the affections of the body may rise to an equality with angelic grace, and grasp the eternity of life."

Clement has strong views on proper clothing. He describes the luxurious materials worn by many—cloth of gold, silk, rich dyes and embroidery, saffron-coloured robes dipped in ointments—all these should be avoided. So too materials so thin that they do not conceal the shape of the body, and those that are so long that they trail on the ground, sweeping up the dirt like a broom. "But for those who are white and unstained within, it is most suitable to wear white and simple garments." Men and women should wear the same kind of clothing, though if some concession is to be made women may have softer garments. Women, too, should wear shoes so long as they are white, and not gold-plated or bejewelled; for a man bare feet are suitable, though if we are on a journey we may use slippers or white shoes.

One of the chapters in *The Pedagogue* is called *Against Embellishing the Body*. Clement begins by describing the Egyptian temples. They have, he says, porticos and vestibules, groves and fields adjoining, halls surrounded with pillars, walls gleaming with gold, silver and amber, and glittering with gems from India and Ethiopia. But if you enter the shrine and lift the veil what do you see? Not the deity you expected, but a cat, a crocodile or a serpent, a creature more suitable to lie in the dirt than to roll on a purple couch. So it is with women. They curl their locks, rub their cheeks with white lead, stain their eyebrows with soot and dye their hair; but if you look within what do you find? Not a virtuous and religious soul but one given up to the lusts of the flesh. Such women spend the whole day shut up with their maids, decking themselves out, and only creep forth at night, when drunkenness and a dim light aid their make-up. And these cosmetics chill the skin, furrow the flesh with poison, turn the complexion yellow, and actually destroy the beauty they are meant to enhance. Nor is it only the women who imagine they embellish themselves by such arts. Men too are to be found who disgrace themselves in the same way. They comb their hair, shave with a razor or remove the hair by the use of pitch, and when they grow old dye their grey hair yellow. The love of luxury has deranged all things—it has disgraced men and women alike.

It was, at that time, the fashion for both men and women to wear wreaths at their banquets. This too Clement disapproves of. Those who crown themselves, he says, destroy the pleasure there is in flowers. Why spoil the natural charm of flowers by making wreaths? In the springtime it is delightful to while away the time in the dewy meadows while soft, many-coloured flowers are in bloom among the bees. But those who wear garlands enjoy neither the sight nor the fragrance, for the crown is worn above the eyes and the nose.

Other objects of luxury against which Clement inveighs are cups made of gold and silver, and inlaid with precious stones. How absurd! for if you pour hot liquid into them you cannot touch them. Away with these goblets—away with silver couches, tripods and ivory, beds studded with tortoise-shell and bed-clothes of purple—all these are signs of tasteless luxury, unfitting to a Christian.

Nor are these the only ways in which money can be wasted. I must, says Clement, find fault with the large numbers of servants some people have. There may be a whole army of cooks—makers of sweetmeats, honey-cakes and custards, special seasoners and carvers. There are some to lay the table, take care of the clothes, polish the silver, rub down the horses, and preside over the toilet of their masters and mistresses. But workers in wool, spinners, weavers, housekeepers, are nowhere to be found. Again, foolish women spend their money on pets—Indian birds, parrots, puppies and apes. They would do better to take into their houses orphan children, and care for the needs of the aged. Who are so poor as the rich who squander their gold and have nothing to give away?

Clement has some excellent hints on good manners in conversation. We ought not, he justly observes, to talk too much —sum up your discourse in a few words. The voice should be modulated and kept from loudness, drawling, rapidity and prolixity. Don't interrupt, or answer before you have heard the question. Refrain from arguing merely for the sake of a useless triumph. Avoid jibing at those with whom you are in company. After all we meet together socially in a friendly spirit, why should we stir up enmity by jibing and puzzling people with difficult questions? We do not like being made ridiculous ourselves and therefore should not make fun of others. A certain amount of pleasantry is however permissible and elder people may sometimes be playful and joke with the young. For instance, a father who has a shy, silent son might say, "This boy of mine is forever chattering." But excessive laughter should be checked—women should not giggle, for it is affected, men should not guffaw or give vent to savage and insulting laughter. But there is no need to be gloomy.

An important feature in the lives of the ancients was, as is well known, the baths. These baths were looked on with horror by devout Christians, nor is this to be wondered at, for, as Clement tells us, they were open promiscuously to men

and women, who appeared before each other stripped naked.
The public baths were, he says, furnished with gold-plated and
silver chairs, braziers of coals, and ten thousand vessels to contain food and drink, "for people have arrived at such a pitch of
self-indulgence that they sup and get drunk while bathing".
These luxurious and indecent habits seem unfortunately to have
caused cleanliness itself to be regarded with suspicion. Clement
shows the beginning of this undesirable attitude by telling us
that "the bath is to be taken by women for cleanliness and
health, by men for health only". This identification of dirt with
holiness soon reached very unpleasant lengths. Clement's
special permission to women to be clean was quickly forgotten.
Saint Paula, a friend of St. Jerome, is reported to have said to
her nuns, "A clean body and a clean dress mean an unclean
soul." "For my part," says St. Jerome, "I disapprove altogether
of baths for adult virgins." The great hermit, St. Anthony, we
are told, never allowed water to touch him. On the other hand
a certain bishop caused considerable scandal by having two
baths every day. When the shocked members of his congregation asked him why he did this he replied coolly, "Because it is
not convenient to have three." We need not add that this
bishop was a heretic.

It must not be supposed that the Pedagogue confines his
instruction to manners. Morals are by no means omitted; the
sins of the flesh—homosexuality, adultery and so forth—
dishonesty, violence, are of course inveighed against. But
there is nothing much to which we need draw particular
attention.

3. STROMATEIS. Clement himself has described this book
as a haphazard collection of notes. "In a meadow," he says,
"we find all sorts of flowers blooming together, in a park
fruit trees are not separated according to species. Many authors
have composed collections of this sort, which they have called
Meadows, Helicons, Honeycombs, Robes." So we too have
our Anthologies, collections of flowers, in which poems by

different authors are put together. It is here that Clement
shows the variety and extent of his learning. He quotes
extensively from biblical and apocryphal sources, from
Gnostic literature, from classical philosophy and poetry. These
quotations preserve many fragments from lost and unknown
books. As he tells us himself, there is but little plan in the book;
it is all "haphazard", full of digressions and even disconnected
sentences. We sense dimly that he wishes to provide the more
advanced Christian with a more profound insight into his
religion; his teaching here approaches the esoteric. There was
a tradition in the early Church that after the Resurrection the
Lord appeared to the Apostles and his most important women
disciples, and taught them a more profound doctrine than is
to be found in the Gospels. This teaching was to be reserved
for those who were specially initiated—it was not for the
ordinary believer. The Gnostics claimed to base their theories
on this orally transmitted doctrine. Clement of course was
violently opposed to these Gnostics, but he certainly held that
a loftier knowledge of holy things raised the learner to a higher
spiritual plane than the simple believer could ever attain. It is
certain that the simple believer will find the *Stromateis* a difficult work to master, and his difficulties will not be diminished
by the frequent harshness of Clement's style and the corrupt
condition of the text that has reached us.

Origen

The life of Origen (c. 185–254) is full of contradictions. The
most famous and successful teacher in the Catechetical School
of Alexandria, he was never ordained there, but was driven
out by the hostility of the bishop Demetrius and spent the
latter part of his life as a presbyter in Caesarea. Loved and
revered in Palestine, Phoenicia, Greece and Arabia, he was
deposed from the rank of presbyter by the two synods con-
vened by the church of Egypt. Consulted and renowned

throughout the East, he was ignored by Rome. Dying, from the effects of a cruel persecution, in full communion with the church, his writings were eventually condemned as heretical. The greatest protagonist of an allegorical interpretation of the scriptures, his literal reading of the text concerning those who make themselves eunuchs for the sake of the kingdom of heaven (Matt. 19: 12) caused him to castrate himself. Recognised today by many of the most learned Roman Catholics as on a par with St. Augustine, and with him the greatest genius of early Christianity, he was never canonised, and still hovers officially on the borders of heresy.

Origen was the first great Christian teacher who was born of a Christian family. As a child he was taught by his father Leonides, who was deeply impressed by his early piety and precocious questioning. Leonides was convinced that his son's body was the dwelling place of the Holy Ghost, and when the child was asleep used reverentially to kiss his bosom, as the priest kisses the altar and the book of the Gospels. Origen was still only a youth when the persecution of Septimus Severus broke out (A.D. 202). Leonides was arrested and threatened with death. Origen was eager to share his martyrdom, and would have given himself up to the prefect had not his mother prevented him from leaving the house, by hiding his clothes. All that Origen could do was to send a letter to his father, urging him to stand firm in the faith, and not to yield out of consideration for his family. Leonides did not disappoint him; he died a martyr's death and as his property was confiscated by the state his widow and family were left destitute.

Origen, the eldest of seven children, was obliged to do what he could to support them. He became a teacher—at first of grammar and Greek literature—and was so successful that he was appointed by Demetrius, the bishop of Alexandria, to the head of the Catechetical School. He thus became the successor of Clement, who by this time had left Alexandria.

He adopted a life of extreme asceticism, and it was at this time that he mutilated himself, a proceeding which he afterwards regretted, and which had an unfortunate effect on his career.

While part of his time was spent in teaching he plunged more and more deeply into the study of philosophy as well as the Scriptures. He was lucky enough to make friends with a wealthy Alexandrian, Ambrosius, and by his help embarked on his great work the *Hexapla*. This was an edition of the Old Testament. It was set out in six parallel columns—the Hebrew text, a Greek transliteration, and four different Greek versions. This was an entirely new idea, and for the first time enabled students to make a serious comparison of the Old Testament texts. Origen was enabled to undertake this colossal labour by the generosity of Ambrosius, who supplied him with manuscripts and put at his disposal seven shorthand writers, to take down from his dictation, and seven scribes to write the matter out. Origen continued to work on the *Hexapla* for thirty years, altering and improving it. Alas, but little remains today of this monumental work. It was too huge to be reproduced, and Origen's copy seems to have perished when the Mohammedans destroyed Caesarea in 653.

On the death of Septimus Severus in 211 the persecution of the Christians stopped. But five years later another blow fell on Alexandria. The Emperor Caracalla, enraged at some personal insults, descended on the city and put to death thousands of the inhabitants. This frenzied massacre, known in history as the Fury of Caracalla, had nothing to do with the Christians, but Alexandria became such a dangerous centre that Origen left it, and removed to Palestine. Here he was eagerly welcomed by the bishops of Jerusalem and Caesarea, who took advantage of his presence to get him to teach in their churches. This gave rise to his difficulties with the bishop of Alexandria to which we have referred and which ended in his settling down as a presbyter in Caesarea. Here he continued for many years, his success and fame increasing year by year. During this period he became the teacher of Gregory Thaumaturgus—the Wonder Worker. Gregory, on leaving Caesarea, composed a Panegyric on Origen, in which he describes his pedagogical methods, and gives a delightful picture of his personal charm, "unspeakably winning, holy, and lovely in the extreme".

Two more persecutions interrupted the serenity of the scholar's life—the first under Maximin, in 235, from which he escaped, by going into hiding, the second under Decius (249-251), to which he fell a victim. He was imprisoned, tortured, and threatened with death at the stake. He held firm, however, and surviving his torments escaped with his life on the death of Decius. His sufferings had, however, worn him out. He seems to have lived another two or three years, and died at Tyre, where a marble monument marked his grave till the end of the thirteenth century.

Origen was one of the most prolific writers who have ever lived. Epiphanius says he composed 6,000 volumes—doubtless small scrolls—and declares that no one can read his complete works. Many of them have now disappeared, but the remaining bulk is very considerable. Very little of it, however, is suitable for quotation here, as it is almost entirely theological and exegetical, and it is impossible to give any idea of his laborious studies and immense learning.

There is another difficulty in dealing with him. One of his major works—*On First Principles*—is only partially extant in the original Greek. In the fourth century Basil the Great and Gregory Nazianzen made a selection from Origen's writings called the *Philocalia*, and this has preserved some passages from the *First Principles*. The rest exists only in Latin translations. Towards the end of the fourth century Origen's reputation had fallen under a cloud; he was violently attacked by Epiphanius, who convinced St. Jerome that his teaching was dangerous. Rufinus, a friend of Jerome's, was partially won over, but finding much that was edifying in *First Principles* he translated it into Latin. His translation was, however, by no means faithful. He omitted, interpolated, and altered the text, so as to keep clear of any suspicion of unorthodoxy. His translation roused Jerome to fury. He made his own version of the text, but this, too, has disappeared, except for a few passages in one of his letters.

Bearing all this in mind it will readily be appreciated that our quotations give but little idea of Origen's profound and encyclopaedic mind—they are merely selected to show some of his less recondite ideas, and the reader is implored not to judge Origen from these few excerpts.

Allegorical interpretation. The Bible, and in particular the Old Testament, is full of statements that have perplexed devout readers. Marcion, perceiving that the God of the Old Testament was described as cruel, jealous and bad tempered, decided that he was not the same as the fatherly God of the New Testament, and called him the Demiurge, or Workman. Origen's method was to explain away difficulties as allegories.

"Will any man of sense," he writes, "suppose that a first, a second and a third day, morning and evening, existed without sun and moon and stars? . . . And who is so silly as to imagine that God, like a husbandman, planted a garden in Eden and put in it a tree of life, which could be seen and felt so that anyone who tasted the fruit with his bodily teeth received the gift of life? . . . Why, even the Gospels are filled with narratives of the same kind. We read of the Devil leading Jesus up on to a high mountain to show him the kingdoms of the world and their glory. Who but a careless reader of these things would not condemn the supposition that with the bodily eye . . . Jesus beheld the kingdoms of Persia, Scythia, India and Parthia and the glory of their rulers among men?"

Origen therefore takes for granted that allegory must be used in the interpretation of Scripture. The method, though so common with the early Fathers, does not meet with approval from all writers. In this way, says a modern Catholic writer, "any doctrine may be discovered in any given text; and thus the door is opened to private judgement, to rash speculation and to all the vagaries of an ever-changing philosophy". Other writers of these days would adduce different objections; from whatever reason, the allegorical method of interpretation is now a thing of the past, and retains only an historical interest.

Magic. "Magic is not, as the Epicureans and Aristotelians suppose, utterly incoherent, but, as the experts prove, a consistent system which has principles known to very few." One of the fundamental principles of magic is, as is well known, the use of the correct names of spiritual beings. "Our Jesus," says Origen, "keeps to the same philosophy of names; for His name has been clearly proved to drive out countless demons from souls and bodies, powerfully working on those from whom they were expelled. And as regards names, we may further observe that experts in the use of charms tell us that if we pronounce a given spell in its own lauguage it can bring about the effect that the charm professes to do; but if we translate it into another language it will be found to be weak and ineffective."

Heavenly Bodies. "Let us see what reason can discover about the sun, moon and stars, whether it is correct to suppose, as some do, that they are exempt from the possibility of change. . . . Now Job appears to show that not only is it possible for the stars to be subject to sins but that they are in fact 'not clean' from the contagion of sin."[1]

"We think therefore that they may be called living beings because they are said to receive commands from God; which is ordinarily the case only with living and rational creatures."

"We are convinced that the sun itself and the moon and stars pray to the supreme God. . . ."

Angels. "The Lord's portion is his people Jacob[2] . . . whereas other nations are said to be the portion of his angels."

---

[1] The stars are not pure in his sight. Job 25: 5.   [2] Deut. 32: 9.

"These shepherds[1] must be considered to be the angels to whom the care of men is entrusted. And each one of these was taking pains to watch over those who were entrusted to him: but they needed help that the nations in their charge should be well guided. It was to them that the angel came to announce the birth of Jesus, and the coming of the True Shepherd."[2]

Universalism. Universalism is the belief that in the end all men will be saved. This, an essential part of Origen's belief, was—and is—violently assailed by orthodox writers.

"Now I myself think that when it is said that 'God will be all in all'[3] it means that he will also be all things in each individual person, and in such a way that everything which the rational mind, when purified from all wickedness, can feel or understand or think will be all God. . . . For there will no longer be any contrast of good and evil, since evil nowhere exists."

Origen carries his thought to its logical conclusion. When "God is all in all", when "evil nowhere exists", Satan too will be saved.

"The last enemy"—death, says Rufinus, but Origen clearly meant and probably said Satan—"will be destroyed not in the sense of ceasing to exist, but of being no longer an enemy. For to the Almighty nothing is impossible, nor is anything beyond the reach of cure by its Maker."

Julius Africanus

Julius Africanus is an unusual and somewhat mysterious figure. He was a contemporary of Origen, with whom he interchanged letters, and was the author of a letter to a certain Aristides, a book on Chronology, and a book of miscellanies

---

[1] On Luke 2: 5. And there were in the same country shepherds abiding in the field keeping watch over their flocks by night.
[2] A typical example of allegorical interpretation.
[3] 1 Cor. 15: 28.

called *Cestoi*, or *Embroidered Girdles*. *Cestoi*, of which fragments only are extant, seems to have contained instructions on agriculture and military affairs; among the latter are directions as to how to poison wells and stores of the enemy's food. It contains also medical hints and charms. To preserve wine, for instance, you should write on the vessel that contains it the words "Taste, and see that the Lord is gracious". Such pieces of information have seemed to some incompatible with a belief in Christianity and they are credited to another author of the same name. Africanus was, however, undoubtedly a man of wide and peculiar interests. He was a native of Palestine and was much travelled. He visited Alexandria, Rome and Edessa. He seems to have been friendly with Abgar, the King of Edessa, a descendant of the Abgar who corresponded with Jesus, with whom he used to go out hunting, and he tells us in his *Chronicon* that there had formerly been preserved there Jacob's tent, which however had been destroyed by lightning. He does not mention the letter of Jesus which we have described elsewhere. He also visited Mount Ararat in Parthia, the place where Noah's Ark made its landfall, and he describes the Dead Sea from personal observation.

Of the *Chronicon* we have but few fragments. It was an attempt to synchronise sacred and profane history and seems to have shown considerable mathematical and astronomical knowledge. The darkness at the time of the Crucifixion must have been miraculous, as an eclipse of the sun cannot take place at the full moon of the Passover.

The *Letter to Aristides* is an attempt to harmonise the genealogies of our Lord given in Matthew and Luke, the discrepancies of which have long been a stumbling block to Biblical critics. Africanus accounts for the differences by saying that "in Israel the names of their generations were enumerated according to nature, or according to law". By "according to law" Africanus alludes to cases where a man married his brother's widow—the so-called Levirate marriage. In this

THE FATHERS WITHOUT THEOLOGY

case the children, though actually those of the woman's second husband, were supposed to be those of the first husband, and in this way a person had at the same time an actual and a legal descent. When he goes into details he becomes somewhat confused, and his explanation has not entirely satisfied modern students.

The *Letter to Origen* is the most interesting of the extant writings of Africanus. It begins by speaking of a discussion between Origen and a certain Bassus, at which Africanus was present. During the discussion Origen mentioned the Story of Susanna, which caused some surprise to Africanus. To make the point clear we must remind the reader that the Book of Daniel as it appears in the Bible is bilingual—it is partly in Hebrew and partly in Aramaic. Moreover the Greek versions contain three groups of material which are neither in the Hebrew nor the Aramaic text: these are the *Song of the Three Children*, the *Story of Susanna*, and the *Story of Bel and the Dragon*, all of which are to be found in our Apocrypha. The early Church, using the Greek versions, accepted these additions as part of the Bible, and it was Origen's acceptance of them that caused the astonishment of Africanus. At the time of the conversation, he says, he thought it only polite to make no protest. "Now, however, I cannot understand how it escaped you that this part of the book is spurious. For in truth this section, though elegantly written, is a mere modern forgery." It was, he argues, written originally in Greek, and much later than the rest of the book. His arguments may be summarised as follows. He finds in the Greek two puns. The elder who says he saw Susanna under a mastich tree (σχῖνον) will be torn asunder (σχίσει); the elder who saw her under a holm oak (πρῖνον) will be sawn apart (καταπρίσῃ). This cannot be a translation from the Hebrew, in which there would be no pun. Moreover the story is not to be found in the Hebrew text. He further assails the subject matter as anachronistic. The Jews, who are all captives, could not possibly

sentence to death the wife of their king Joakin—or if this is
some Joakin of lower rank, how comes he to possess a spacious
mansion and garden? "Moreover," he concludes, "the style
is different from the rest of the Book of Daniel. From all this
I infer that this section is a later addition. I have struck the
blow; answer and instruct me. The learned all salute thee.
With all my heart I pray for you and your friends' health."

Origen was not convinced by these arguments. "The
passage," he says, concerning the names of the trees, "gave
me no rest, and I often wondered about it, so I consulted several
Jews on the matter. . . . They said they did not know the
Greek words and asked me to show them the trees, that they
might see what they called them. And I at once (for truth's
dear sake) put before them pieces of the different trees." The
Jews, however, gave evasive answers, and were obviously
quite unfamiliar with the plants. "I am therefore cautious,"
Origen continues, "of affirming whether there is any similar
play of words in the Hebrew. Your reason for affirming there
is not you yourself probably know." The reason the passage
is not found in Hebrew is that the Jews deliberately cut out
many things from the Bible, especially such as contained scandal against the rulers and judges. "Your last objection," he
winds up, "is that the style is different. This I cannot see."

Most modern scholars are of opinion that the story was
originally written in Aramaic and that the pun was made by
using the names of other trees. The other objections made by
Africanus are thought to be valid, and the passage is now dated
between 95 and 80 B.C.—about a hundred years after the Book
of Daniel.

V

The Organized Church

WE have now reached the third century A.D. and by this time the Christian Church is beginning to be organized as a unified and self-conscious entity. The theologians are providing her with an elaborated system of thought which eventually formed the basis of Catholicism. Those who adhered to this system called themselves Orthodox; those outside it they called Heretics.

At the same time what we may call the political development of the Church was taking place. The centre of gravity was passing gradually from the East to the West. Rome was increasing in importance, and almost suddenly, towards 200, the Western Church abandoned Greek and began the use of Latin for liturgical and religious purposes. The relations of the Bishop of Rome with other bishops came under consideration, the discipline of the Church was gradually defined and narrowed, and for the first time schisms are found, the members of which broke away from the Orthodox church, not because they held heretical views but because they had their own ideas as to Church management and discipline. Hippolytus, Tertullian and Novatian were among the first schismatics, and Hippolytus is thought by some modern authors to have been the first anti-pope.

Without entering into the minutiae of heresies we shall glance at some of the curious ideas of the schismatics, and recount some of the surprising episodes arising from the disputes among notable churchmen.

We begin this section, therefore, with a review of affairs in the chief centres of the Western Church—Rome and Carthage.

The Story of Pope Callistus

A success story is always popular, and no doubt has an added piquancy if it is related by the mortal enemy of the hero. Hippolytus, one of the early Fathers who lived in Rome towards the year 200, nourished a bitter hatred for Pope Callistus, and poured his venom into his book *Refutation of All Heresies*. In this work, besides attacking the Pope's orthodoxy, he gives a short and malignant biography of his enemy. Unfortunately we have no means of checking the veracity of his account, as the only other contemporary writer from whom we hear of Callistus is Tertullian, who vied with Hippolytus in malevolence towards him. The story in any case is a curious one, and after the lapse of 1,800 years may be read with less rancorous feelings than those that inspired it.

In the time of Marcus Aurelius, during the pontificate of Eleutherus, there lived a certain Carpophorus of the household of Caesar. Carpophorus was a Christian and a man of position, owning a considerable number of slaves, among them the Christian, Callistus. Carpophorus seems to have had a number of irons in the fire—one of his enterprises was a bank, situated on the site of the Baths of Caracalla. Callistus was sent to take charge of this bank, and was entrusted with funds for the purpose. Whether from roguery or bad management the funds disappeared, the bank failed and a horde of furious creditors appeared on the scene. Callistus, terrified at the thought of his fate if he were to fall into the hands of his master, fled from Rome to Portus, the nearest point of embarkation, and found a ship which he hoped would carry him to some safe refuge. To his horror, just before the ship sailed, he caught sight of Carpophorus, who had discovered his flight, and tracked him to the port. Callistus lost his head. The fate of a slave, fugitive and recaptured, might indeed be terrible, and Callistus felt that drowning was preferable to crucifixion. He

leapt into the sea, but the crowded harbour was full of interested spectators, and he was quickly fished out again, and
handed over to his master. Carpophorus, though justly
indignant, remembered that he was a Christian, and refrained
from inflicting the worst penalty on the criminal. He sent
him to the *pistrinum*, a mill, worked by the forced labour of
the lowest slaves sentenced to punishment.

The fate of Callistus, though doubtless gratifying to his
creditors, did not appease them. They wanted their money.
Many of them were Christians, and they besieged Carpophorus
with demands for repayment. He, however, knew little or
nothing about the affairs of the bank. He was obliged to
consult Callistus, who eagerly informed him that money was
owing to the bank, which he could in all probability recover,
and with which he might satisfy the clamouring creditors.
Carpophorus was persuaded to release him on the understanding that he would duly collect these moneys.

Callistus no doubt congratulated himself at his escape from
prison; it proved, however, only the beginning of worse
misfortunes. The most important of the debtors to the bank
were Roman Jews, and to them Callistus determined to apply.
The moment he chose for approaching them was unfortunately
ill-timed. He entered the synagogue while the Jews were
conducting a religious ceremony, and their fury at the profane
approach of a debt-collector at such a moment may be well
imagined. The synagogue was immediately in a violent
uproar, and the outraged Jews haled Callistus before the
Roman Prefect, Fuscianus, before whom they laid their complaint. Carpophorus hurried to the defence of his slave, and
seems to have pacified the Jews. But in the course of enquiries
into the case Fuscianus discovered that the unfortunate Callistus
was a Christian, and sentenced him to be deported to Sardinia
to work there in the silver-mines.

These events took place in the year 187. In 180 Marcus
Aurelius, one of the best Roman Emperors, died, and was

F 161

succeeded by his son Commodus, one of the worst. Marcus Aurelius was a great persecutor of the Christians, but Commodus, except for a few sporadic attacks at the beginning of his reign, left them alone. This was apparently owing to the influence of his chief concubine, Marcia. Marcia's life was a strange one. She was educated by a certain Christian Hyacinthus, a eunuch, and yet we are told a presbyter. Before entering the harem of Commodus she was in turn the mistress of Quadratus who was murdered by Commodus, and of Eclectus, the lover first of Quadratus and then of Commodus. She was however a Christian, and successfully protected her co-religionists against the bloodthirsty Emperor. In 190 Pope Eleutherus died, and was succeeded by Victor. Marcia took the opportunity of obtaining from Commodus a pardon for the Christians doing forced labour in Sardinia, and applied to the Pope for a list of their names. Victor furnished her with a list from which, perhaps by chance, but more probably by design, he omitted the name of Callistus. Marcia dispatched Hyacinthus to Sardinia, armed with the list, and only when he arrived in Sardinia did he discover that the name of Callistus was not among the pardoned. Hyacinthus, ignorant doubtless of the past history of Callistus, persuaded the procurator that the omission was a mere slip, secured his release with the other Christians, and brought the whole party back to Rome. The return of Callistus proved an embarrassment to the Pope. His presence in Rome was an annoyance to the other Christians and a blot on the purity of the church. Victor therefore sent him to Antium and paid him a small monthly pension on condition he did not return to Rome.

Three years after these events Commodus met with his death. Marcia and Eclectus came by chance on a list of those who were to be executed on the following day, in which, to their horror, they found their own names included. They at once resolved to anticipate their fate, and administered a draft of poison to the Emperor. The poison did not take immediate effect, but when Commodus was in his bath he fell into a stupor. Marcia and Eclectus, to make certain of their work, called in a young and powerful wrestler, who quietly strangled the unconscious tyrant.

There followed some months of confusion. Marcia disappeared from the scene and when eventually Septimus Severus became Emperor toleration too disappeared, and the peace and prosperity of the Empire were accompanied by new persecutions of the Christians.

Meanwhile Pope Victor died and was succeeded by Zephyrinus. This was the opportunity of Callistus. During his banishment at Antium he had devoted himself to study and had become a deacon. Zephyrinus immediately summoned him to Rome and the evil days of Callistus were over. His foot was on the ladder which led him to the crown of a Pope and the halo of a saint. He was first of all entrusted with the charge of the Roman cemeteries. These cemeteries were of the utmost importance to the Christian communities—they were their assembly rooms, their only churches, as well as their burial places, and formed indeed the centres of their cult. Callistus moved the cemetery, then on Via Salaria, to the Appian Way, where it became known as the Cemetery of Callistus. That was, however, far from being his most important concern. He soon became the chief adviser of Pope Zephyrinus, who seems to have been a simple soul, with not much theological knowledge and a great desire to maintain the peace of the Church. This being his object, his lines were indeed cast in an unfortunate time and place. Rome was a centre to which flocked every kind of religious theoriser, bringing in his train innumerable heresies and schisms. One of these heresiarchs—Theodotus—had already been excommunicated by Pope Victor. He had, however, been able to organise a church of his own, amongst whose bishops was a certain Roman priest, Natalius. After the death of Victor, Natalius had a terrible vision. The Lord appeared to him and delivered a stinging rebuke; nor did He stop at words, but summoned a troop of holy angels who spent the night in inflicting on the peccant priest an even more painful bodily chastisement. When daybreak rescued him from these angelic tormentors the unhappy Natalius staggered to the throne of Pope Zephyrinus, cast himself weeping at his feet, and implored forgiveness. Zephyrinus took pity on the sinner, and eventually readmitted him to communion.

But there were other, greater problems awaiting the judgement of the Pope. The mystery of the Trinity was beginning to be investigated and was already leading to bitter disputes and recriminations. There were the Montanists, of whom we shall speak more fully in another chapter. They brought into prominence the somewhat neglected Person of the Holy Ghost.

The second Person of the Trinity also gave rise to varying teachings. Those who were called Modalists declared that there was but one God, who himself was incarnate in Jesus Christ. Their opponents seemed to fall into the opposite error of maintaining the existence of *two* Gods—the Father and the Son. Zephyrinus found himself on the horns of a dilemma. He would not condemn the Modalists, for how could he deny that there was but one God? Tertullian, who hated the Modalists as much as he reverenced the Montanists, declared bitterly that in Rome Satan had won two great victories. He put to flight the Paraclete and crucified the Father. This saying had a great success, and the enemies of the Modalists called them in mockery the Patripassionists.

Among the most eminent of these enemies was Hippolytus, a stern, puritanical theologian who in Rome opposed the Pope with as much fury as Tertullian did in Africa. Nor was he appeased by the death of Zephyrinus. Zephyrinus was succeeded by Callistus, and Hippolytus had long since detected beneath the robes of the wavering Zephyrinus the sinister figure of the former fugitive slave. Protesting violently against the scandal of such an elevation he withdrew from communion with the Church, and though Callistus finally excommunicated the Modalists as heretics, Hippolytus maintained his schismatic position.

The new Pope was perhaps not unduly troubled by the secession of Hippolytus. At any rate he continued on a path which called forth new revilings from his opponent. In a spirit of mildness and perhaps from practical policy, he re-formed the discipline of the Church. It had long been held that adulterers, murderers and apostates must be excommuni-cated and could never obtain absolution. This doctrine, as the Church spread and times changed, could not be persisted in. Callistus took the first step by receiving back into the Church penitent adulterers. This further enraged the puritanical Hippolytus and Tertullian, and Hippolytus accuses him in addition of other fatal ways of relaxing Church discipline. He seems to have refused to suspend peccant bishops, to have allowed the clergy to marry, and even to have tolerated secret marriages between Roman ladies of good family and men of the lower orders—even slaves, for Callistus could not forget that he himself had been a slave. These were the crimes which caused Hippolytus to throw away all discretion, and publish to the world the infamy of the Pope in his *Refutation of All Heresies*.

Callistus only occupied the chair of St. Peter for three years; but his end is veiled in mystery. He was canonised in the time of Constantine the Great as a martyr; but at the time of his death the Church was at peace—no persecutions were in progress. His death cannot be attributed to his experiences in the Sardinian mines, for thirty years had passed since that unfortunate episode. Moreover, he alone of the third-century Popes was not buried in the cemetery on the Appian Way— his own cemetery. He was buried in the Via Aurelia, in a poor district of Rome, and it has been suggested that he lost his life in an anti-Christian riot of the local ruffians. It is all conjecture;

but doubtless his true end was not there, but in the glorious heaven of the noble army of martyrs.

Hippolytus

Hippolytus was a saint, a martyr, and the first anti-pope. We have seen how he withdrew from communion with Callistus, who, however, never excommunicated him. He remained the leader of a schismatic sect under the next two Popes, Urban and Pontian, and his followers recognised him as the Bishop of Rome. It has been plausibly suggested that his congregation consisted of the Greek-speaking Christians of Rome, while Callistus presided over those who spoke Latin. These were, however, the more numerous, and were growing in numbers, while those who held to Greek were every day becoming fewer. It is indeed towards this time that Greek, hitherto the only language of the Church, was in Rome replaced by Latin. Latin rapidly became the medium of theological writings and church liturgies. A rift was made between the East and the West, which led finally to a separation between the Catholic Church, centred in Rome, and the Orthodox Church, centred in Constantinople.

Hippolytus was undoubtedly a remarkable man. He was a famous preacher. Origen, on a visit to Rome, attended one of his sermons, and Hippolytus recognised him and alluded to his presence.

He wrote many books of exegesis, a book on the origin of evil, on the substance of the universe and on the resurrection. He also concerned himself with the Paschal Question,[1] and drew up tables by which its date was to be determined. A statue was erected to him, which still exists, though with a modern head. Hippolytus is represented as seated on an episcopal throne; around the base are engraved the Easter Tables and a list of his writings. This statue was rediscovered in

[1] *V.* p. 31; 34 a.

the sixteenth century; it appears to have been originally set up in 222, the year in which Callistus died.

Hippolytus was much interested in heresies, as we see from the title of his great book *Refutation of All Heresies*. Much of it is based on Irenaeus; but it does not deal exclusively with heresy. As we have seen it contains a diatribe against Callistus, also some inaccurate accounts of Greek philosophers, and a chapter exposing the tricks of magicians. This chapter is especially interesting, as it was commonly believed by Christians—including Origen—that the marvels performed by conjurers were done by the aid of demons. Hippolytus, who seems to have had some knowledge of chemistry, exposes them as impostures. These are some of the tricks he describes.

"Thunder is produced in many ways. Large stones rolled from a height over wooden planks and falling upon sheets of brass make a noise very like thunder. And they coil a slender cord round a thin board . . . and then spin the board by whisking away the string, when its whirring makes the sound of thunder."

A magician will plunge his hands into a cauldron of boiling pitch and walk bare foot on coals of fire without hurting himself. He manages in this way. The magician sets a cauldron of pitch over a fire, and throws in nitre (or soda) and vinegar. A small amount of heat will cause the vinegar to bubble and make it appear to be boiling, and if he smears his hands with myrtle-juice, nitre (soda) and myrrh he will not even scorch his hands by dipping them in the pitch. Similarly, if he smears his feet with fish glue and powdered salamander he can walk on live coals without pain.

Other chapters deal with such matters as Method of Poisoning Goats; How to make Sheep Behead Themselves; How to Open and Reseal Sealed Letters; How to Produce the Illusion of Fiery Demons. The story of Apsethus, another impostor, is amusing.

"Apsethus the Libyan yearned to become a god. But when

after repeated manœuvres he failed in his attempt, he wished at all events to appear to have become one, and seemed as if he might really achieve this in time." He collected a great number of parrots, and having shut them up in a cage he taught them to say 'Apsethus is a god.' He then let them out and they flew in all directions and settled on the tops of trees, whence they repeated their lesson. "The foolish Libyans, thinking that they must believe voices which appeared to come from heaven above, sacrificed to him as to some divine power." A sceptical Greek, however, suspected some trickery. He caught the parrots, put them back in a cage, and taught them to say: 'Apsethus shut us up and compelled us to say "Apsethus is a god." ' When the Libyans heard the recantation of the parrots they realised they had been taken in, and rushing in a body on Apsethus they burned him alive.

It is thought by some authors that the quarrel between Hippolytus and the legitimate Pope was healed by their suffering under persecution. During the reign of Maximin the Christians, and especially the clergy, were once more attacked. The legitimate Pope Pontian and the anti-Pope Hippolytus were both seized and sent to the Sardinian mines. There they made up their differences and became reconciled. Both Popes died on the island; after the death of Maximin their bodies were brought back to the mainland and interred in the catacombs of Rome.

A Vanished Sect—The Montanists

Among the many oriental rites performed to secure successful harvests and increased fertility, we find a curious group of beliefs closely resembling each other and often confused. The myths developed from these rituals spoke of a Mother goddess often associated with the death of her castrated son on a tree, and the priests who performed the ceremonies were themselves castrated. One of the most widespread of these myths was that of Cybele and Attis, which reached Rome in 204 B.C. and flourished there for more than 500 years. The festival of Cybele was held towards the end of March, and was accompanied by various processions and orgiastic rites, in which the emasculated priests, Corybantes or Galli, as they were called, accompanied by clashing cymbals, rolling drums, horns and flutes, lashed themselves into frenzy and ecstasy. The home of this belief was Phrygia, where every spring the death of Attis was celebrated with these same orgiastic rites.

Christianity must have reached Phrygia early, for it was one of the districts missionised by St. Paul. It may well be believed that the worship of Attis was frowned upon by the Church, in spite of the curious resemblance between the Christian ceremonies of Good Friday and Easter, and the spring festival of the Corybantes. Nor is it easy to eradicate from the minds of new converts their old inclinations and habits. At any rate there seems to have been a section of Christians in the second century who retained the practice of ecstasy, and if not of castration laid unusual stress on asceticism and virginity.

Towards the end of the second century this movement attained a sudden prominence in the Christian world. There appeared on the scenes a certain Montanus. He was newly baptised and had formerly been a heathen priest—doubtless a priest of Attis. His teaching was severely ascetic, and he was in the habit of falling into frenzies in which he appeared to be possessed by the Spirit of God.

"Behold!" he cried. "The man is like a lyre, and I strike the strings like a plectrum. The man sleeps and I wake. Behold! It is the Lord who moves the heart of man."

In his ecstatic condition he made further announcements. "I am the Lord God, born among men." "I am neither an angel nor a priest. I am God the Father, come to you." "I am the Father, the Son and the Paraclete."

His success in Phrygia was immediate. Two women, Prisca

and Maximilla, soon discovered that they too were vehicles for the voice of God.

"Do not hear me, but hear Christ." "They call me a wolf. I am not a wolf, I am the Voice and the Spirit and the Power."

Such were the utterances of the inspired, and they carried conviction to many.

The centres of their worship were two small towns in Phrygia, Pepusa and Tyana, which Montanus called Jerusalem, and where, he said, the New Jerusalem would shortly descend bodily from heaven, for the end of the world was at hand. Great crowds assembled here, and special ceremonies were performed. Maximilla appeared gorgeously dressed, and wearing golden sandals, a troop of virgins all in white, bearing lamps in their hands, entered the church in procession. They prophesied to the congregation, and weeping profusely, incited them to repentance. The audience too was moved to tears, and after a scene of feverish excitement all partook of Communion.

It is to be noted that the Montanists were not heretics. They held all the correct dogmas of the Church, they preached purity and asceticism, and their fasts were longer and more frequent than was customary. But they maintained that the teaching of the Gospel was not complete. The Holy Ghost, inspirer of all prophets, was manifesting himself in Montanus. They considered that prophets were superior to bishops and they denounced the official leaders of the Church as lax and untrue to the message they had received.

We shall not perhaps be surprised at the reaction of the Church to the New Revelation, as the Montanists called it. Their fury knew no bounds, and they poured out a flood of denunciations and accusations, many of which appear to have been ill-founded. The Montanists were "poisonous reptiles crawling over Asia and Phrygia". Montanus "in the unbounded lust of his soul for leadership gave himself up to the Adversary,

became obsessed and suddenly fell into frenzy and convul-
sions". The orthodox, indeed, fully believed that Montanus
was possessed by a Spirit, but it was not the Holy Spirit—it
was the Devil. "He was possessed by a devil and by a spirit of
error." "He began with voluntary ignorance, but turned to
involuntary madness of soul." That is to say that by deliberately
falling into a trance he allowed Satan to seize possession of
him.

By many signs you might know that they are false prophets.
"Tell me," says Miltiades, a contemporary opponent of Montanus, "tell me, does a prophet dye his hair? Does he pencil his
eyelids? Does he love ornaments? Does he gamble and
dice? Does he lend money? Let them state whether these
things are right or not, and I will show that they have been
done among them."

Another proof of their iniquity is the fact that those they
claim as wonderworkers and martyrs are far from being
martyrs—they are rank impostors. A certain Theodotus, we
are told, "was sometimes taken up and raised to Heaven, when
he fell into a trance and trusted himself to the spirit of deceit,
but was hurled down and died miserably". (This sounds like a
reminiscence of the story of Simon Magus.) Themiso, "who
was garbed with specious covetousness" after being put in
prison for his faith, could not endure his sufferings "but exchanged prison for wealth". (How he did this is obscure. Was
he bribed?) Of course he ought to have been modest about
these proceedings, but he boasted that he was a martyr and,
in imitation of St. Paul, wrote an epistle to the whole Church,
to instruct those whose faith was better than his own. Worst of
all is the case of Alexander, who seems to have lived with
Themiso, with whom he joined in revels. He calls himself a
martyr because he was imprisoned by the Proconsul of
Ephesus. But actually he was condemned not as a Christian,
but for robbery, and he was an old offender. The Christians
managed to get him released, but his own diocese would not

receive him, because of his criminal record. Eusebius, who collected these and many other scandalous stories, seems to have forgotten the story of the Lyons martyrs, though he himself recorded it. In 177, when Marcus Aurelius was Emperor, between forty and fifty Christians were seized, imprisoned, tortured, and finally thrown to the wild beasts in the arena. Among them were many Montanists, who during all their sufferings were in perfect amity with the others and died at last "not leaving pain to their mother the Church, nor sedition and war to the brethren, but joy and peace and concord and love". So the survivors of the Lyons persecution wrote to the brethren in Asia and Phrygia, with the very purpose of allaying the disputes about Montanism that were disturbing the peace of the Church. Eusebius quotes the letter in full. How came he to forget it, in his venomous account of Montanism?

The orthodox found fault with these ecstatics on further grounds. Their ministers were paid—it was not long before all Christian ministers were paid. Their fasts were too long— long and severe fasts soon became a sign of saintliness in the Church. They were said, somewhat mysteriously, to "annul marriage". It is not clear whether this means to forbid second marriages or to recommend the married to abstain from intercourse. In any case both these ideas were later taken up and encouraged by the Church. But the most outrageous calumny against them was the accusation that in their celebration of the Eucharist they killed and ate infants. This infamous slander had long been spread abroad by the heathen against the whole body of Christians, and the Church should have been ashamed of recalling it against their own co-religionists.[1]

It was perhaps the wild scenes of trance and ecstatic utterance that most outraged the susceptibilities of the non-Montanists. They made a determined effort to exorcise Maximilla, a party

---

[1] Nor were they ashamed later of making a similar accusation against the Jews. The charge against them of committing ritual murder persisted, in spite of constant proofs to the contrary, right down to the nineteenth century.

of bishops visiting Tyana for this express purpose. Not unnaturally her admirers intervened, and drove off the frustrated bishops. It was at this moment that Maximilla cried out, "I am driven away like a wolf from the flock. I am not a wolf."

Eventually Montanus and Maximilla died, and the story was circulated that like Judas they had committed suicide. Prisca seems to have survived them some time and about her death we are told nothing. Before 198 the Montanists had been condemned by several Asiatic synods, so that they broke away and formed their own church. So far Montanism was known of chiefly in Asia, but towards A.D. 200 Proclus, a Montanist emissary from the East, arrived in Rome, bringing the New Revelation with him. During the Papacy of Zephyrinus we hear of a formal dispute between Proclus and Gaius, a representative of orthodoxy. But Montanism had no success in Rome, and rapidly disappeared. They prospered more in Africa, where the great Tertullian joined their ranks.

The sect of the Montanists lingered on for another two hundred years. But they were doomed to extinction and oblivion. In Africa they had vanished by St. Augustine's day. In the East, the home of their origin, we find Epiphanius, towards the end of the fourth century, still accusing them of ritual murder, and so too Cyril of Jerusalem, at about the same date. "This Montanus," he says in one of his sermons, "who was out of his mind and really mad, dared to say he was himself the Holy Ghost, he, a miserable man and filled with all uncleanness and lasciviousness; it is enough merely to hint at this, out of respect for the women who are present. . . . He cut the throats of little children and chopped them up into unholy food, for the purpose of their so-called mysteries." Instigated by the Church the Emperors pursued them with increasing violence. In 398 an edict forbade their assemblies in town or country, ordered their meeting houses to be confiscated, their books to be sought out and burnt, while any who concealed them were to be executed. In 407 Theodosius decreed that they, together with Manichees and Priscillianists, were to be put to death. They managed to exist for some time, fugitive and concealed, but by the sixth century all trace of them had disappeared.

Tertullian

Tertullian, like Origen, stands on the outskirts of the Church; but he is in a way the Greek Father's converse. Origen lived and died in communion with the Church; after his death his works were condemned. Tertullian's writings were accepted as orthodox, but he himself, though not a heretic, left the Catholic Church and joined the schismatic sect of Montanists. In spite of this, his influence on the Church of the West has been immense. He was the first—if we except the doubtful Minucius Felix—to write in Latin. His two great successors in Africa, Cyprian and Augustine, were his spiritual heirs. Cyprian is said to have read every day a chapter of Tertullian, whom he called "The Teacher"; he used to say to his assistant, "Da mihi magistrum"—"Give me the teacher". Augustine was influenced both directly by Tertullian himself, and indirectly through Cyprian, whom he greatly admired; thus, through Augustine, Tertullian's thought has continued to impress itself on Western Christianity.

Tertullian was the son of a centurion of the proconsular cohort. In his youth he studied literature, medicine and law, and was for some time in Rome. We do not know when he was converted to Christianity. The first African Christians we know of were the Scillitan martyrs, who suffered in 180 at Carthage. It may well have been the sight of their constancy that caused him to turn to Christianity—he is the author of the celebrated saying: "The blood of the Christians is the seed of the Church." Once converted he took up the defence of his creed with unflagging zeal, and for twenty years poured out a torrent of writings. He wrote against the heathen, the Jews, the heretics, and eventually against the Church and the Pope. He seems to have been for ever in a rage, and his red-hot fury is enlivening if not pleasing. In his vehemence he sometimes seems to stammer with impatience and his language is often turgid and obscure, though from time to time he flashes out striking or paradoxical statements. "The Son of God died: it must be believed because it is absurd. And he was buried and rose again: the fact is certain because it is impossible." "Lie to be true." "God is great when he is small." "The unity of heretics is schism."

He is not entirely without his softer moments, and when he forgets his enemies and their enormities he can be poetical and gentle.

The resurrection of the body. "Day dies into night and is everywhere buried in darkness. The glory of the world is shrouded in gloom, everything is tarnished with blackness. All things become sordid, silent, senseless. Thus the loss of light is mourned. And yet again it revives, with its own beauty, its own dowry, its own sun, the same as before, whole and unimpaired: slaying its own slayer, death, tearing open its own sepulchre, darkness, reappearing as heir to itself, until night also comes to life again, it too accompanied by its own retinue. For the rays of the stars which had been quenched by the light of morning are re-kindled; the absent constellations, which time had removed from sight, are brought back to view; the mirrors of the moon, worn away by her monthly course, are restored to fullness. Winters and summers, springs and autumns, come back again, with their strength, their characteristics, their fruits. The earth too receives instruction from heaven to reclothe the bare trees, to colour the flowers afresh, to spread out the grass again, to reproduce the very seeds that have been devoured, and all this only after they have been consumed. Wonderful plan! first a cheat, then a preserver, to restore it kills, to guard it destroys, to increase it lessens.... All creation is in a state of renewal. Whatever you meet has existed before; whatever you have lost will return again. Everything comes a second time, all things begin when they have passed away, nothing perishes but that it may be recovered. All this revolving order of things is evidence of the resurrection of the dead."

On Prayer. "The angels pray; every creature prays. Cattle and wild beasts pray and bend their knees, and when they issue from their lairs and dens they look up towards heaven, their mouths busily murmuring in their own fashion. Even the birds, rising from their nests, rise up heavenwards, and instead of arms extend their wings in the shape of a cross and utter what seems a prayer."

This most impatient of men wrote a treatise on Patience, which rightly opens with an apology.

"I fully confess to the Lord God that it is rash of me, not to say impudent, to dare to compose a treatise on patience, which I myself am quite unfit to practise." His unfitness, indeed, soon shows itself.

"No doubt the reason anyone hurts you is that you may be pained, because the hurter's enjoyment consists in the pain of the hurt. When then you have upset his enjoyment by not being pained he in his turn will be pained by the loss of his enjoyment. Then you not only go away unhurt, which alone is a satisfaction, but into the bargain you are gratified by your adversary's disappointment and revenged by his pain. This is the utility and pleasure of patience." The moral seems to be, "Do good that evil may come." And of course he cannot forbear to quote, "Vengeance is mine, saith the Lord, I will repay."

At first orthodox, about 207 Tertullian joined the sect of the Montanists. He was led to do this, partly by his innate ascetic character, partly by his admiration for the prophets and the New Revelation, partly, no doubt, by his violent temperament and readiness to oppose the official Church.

Ecstatic visions and prophetic utterances took place in Africa as well as in Phrygia. They were apparently part of the church service, and Tertullian gives a curious description of how the prophecies were delivered. "We have among us," he writes, "a sister whose lot it has been to be favoured with sundry gifts of revelation, which she experiences in the spirit by ecstatic vision amidst the sacred rites of the Lord's Day, in church. She converses with angels, and sometimes even with the Lord. She both sees and hears mysterious communications. Some men's hearts she understands and to them that are in need she distributes remedies. . . . After the people are dismissed, at the conclusion of the sacred services she is in the regular habit of reporting to us whatever she has seen in vision." This sister had often seen people's souls in bodily shape. The soul could be "grasped by the hand and was soft and transparent, of an ethereal colour, and exactly resembled a human being in every respect." It will be observed that the manifestations of the Spirit were on a more modest scale than in Phrygia. Those who were inspired did not declare that they themselves spoke with the voice of God, they merely reported their conversations with angels, or the Lord. The services they held, too, appear to have been the ordinary church services—there were no weeping virgins, no white robes, no torches, and the prophets made their reports more discreetly, not to the whole congregation, but "after the people are dismissed"—presumably to the church officials who might be trusted with such moving messages.

Tertullian gives us a detailed defence of the Montanist teaching. We have a tract by him on Fasting, in which he defends the long fasts they practised. The very formation of the body shows the dangers of eating too much—the belly and the private parts are found side by side—first greed, then lust. During a fast food should be only just sufficient, and it should be *dry*, unmoistened by meat or succulent fruits, and the bath should be avoided as "congruent with a dry diet". He is of course a strong supporter of chastity, and though he himself was married he looked on marriage with a disapproving eye. It is true St. Paul says, "It is better to marry than to burn"; but that does not prove that marriage is right. It is better to lose one eye than two; but you cannot argue from that that it is a good thing to have only one eye. He was violently opposed to second marriages, and even before becoming a Montanist wrote two letters to his wife, urging her not to remarry if he were to die. He is very much preoccupied with the question of dress, and writes a fiercely jocose tract urging men to wear the *pallium*, a cloak worn by philosophers, and not at all favoured by smart young men. Of course women's dress is even more severely treated. On the question of veils he is very decided. All women are to wear them when they leave their houses, and the veils must be long enough to cover the neck. "The region of the veil is co-extensive with the space covered by the hair when unbound," he says, and tells how a sister was chastised by an angel, who beat her uncovered neck, saying sarcastically, "Elegant neck! How right of you to be bare! Why not unveil yourself right down to the loins?" This question of veils was really a matter of dispute at the time. In the East, especially in Egypt, all respectable women wore veils, but not in the West, and Tertullian's views caused a good deal of ill-feeling among women. Of course he is violently opposed to dyeing the hair and making up the face, and even protests against any jewellery. Pearls are merely the diseases of oysters, many gems, it is well known, come from the heads of dragons; how is it possible for Christian women to wear such monstrosities? Even dyed garments come under his reprobation. If God had wanted us to wear coloured clothes, he could easily have created sheep with crimson or sky-blue fleeces.

His opposition to public amusements was more reasonable. The games in the arena were certainly cruel and revolting, the performances in the theatre were often lewd, and both arena and theatre were under the patronage of heathen gods. But in reality it was any pleasure that his puritanical mind condemned.

The mere fact that anything was pleasurable was a sign that it emanated from the Devil. "Nobody," he says, "dilutes poison with gall and hellebore—the accursed thing is put into condiments that are well-seasoned and sweet." So too, the Devil puts into the deadly draught things that appear to be agreeable and innocent. "Let us mourn," he cries, "while the heathen are merry. Life's pleasures are not really pleasures. What greater pleasure is there than the distaste of pleasure?" There is, however, one spectacle which Christians may properly enjoy. "What excites my admiration? . . . Which sight gives me joy? Which arouses me to exultation?" It is the sight that will unfold itself on the last day, when "I see so many illustrious monarchs groaning in the lowest darkness", proconsuls who persecuted Christians, in fires more fierce than those in which they burnt them, philosophers covered with shame before those they deluded, as one fire consumes them. "I shall have a better opportunity then of hearing the tragedians, of viewing the actors in the dissolving flame, of viewing the charioteer all glowing in his chariot of fire, of witnessing the wrestlers, not in their gymnasia, but tossing in the fiery billows." Such are the scenes in which a Christian may take a legitimate, a holy pleasure.

Martyrs and Apostates

Shortly after the death of Pontian and Hippolytus in the Sardinian mines (236), Cyprian became Bishop of Carthage, and Fabian, designated by a dove alighting on his head, was elected Pope. Fabian was soon able to attend to questions of orthodoxy. He was disquieted as to the correctness of Origen's views, and Origen wrote to him, defending himself. His writings, he said, had been falsified, and the Pope was being misled. Fabian was apparently satisfied and the matter was dropped. In Africa the bishop of Lambusis, a certain Privatus, was found guilty of heresy and expelled from the Church. Another person who afterwards became famous was Novatian;

he was ordained by Fabian, but his ordination caused a certain amount of scandal. The circumstances of his baptism were not altogether satisfactory. He had been baptised only on a sick bed, when he was thought to be dying—he had in fact received what was known as *clinical baptism*. Baptism, of course, wiped out all past sin. If one died immediately after baptism one was secure of heaven, but to delay till the last moment was in the nature of a gamble. One might be cut off unexpectedly, and die in all one's iniquity—and then what? The whole situation was, however, fraught with danger, for it was almost impossible to obtain forgiveness for post-baptismal sins. Various concessions to human frailty were gradually introduced. Hermas[1] allowed a second repentance, and this was often admitted for venial sins. Callistus, as we have seen,[2] even allowed it for sins of the flesh, if such wretched sinners were truly repentant. But the conditions were hard. The penitents must first make public confession of their sin in church, then they must come "to make open supplication to the assembly. Behold him now, clothed in a hair shirt, covered with ashes, in a sad plight, a spectacle to excite horror in the hearts of all present. He prostrates himself in the midst of the congregation, before the widows, before the priests, he seizes the fringe of their garments, he kisses their foot-prints, he takes hold of their knees". He might—if his sin had been adultery or the like—be then received back into the church; and this concession appeared to Hippolytus and Tertullian abominable laxity. But for murderers and apostates matters were even worse. For them there remained the discipline known as *exomologesis*, which Tertullian describes in detail.

"Exomologesis is a discipline for man's prostration and humiliation. . . . With regard to dress and food it commands the penitent to lie in sackcloth and ashes, to cover his body with rags of mourning. . . moreover, to know no food and drink but such as is plain . . . for the most part, however, to feed prayers

[1] *V*. p. 22.　　[2] *V*. p. 165.

on fasting, to groan, to weep and make outcries to the Lord; to bow before the feet of the presbyters and kneel to God's dear ones; to enjoin on all the brethren to bear his deprecatory supplications before God." All this *may* win God's forgiveness, but it will never secure re-admission into the Church. To the end of his life the sinner must be an outcast, rejected from the sacraments, spurned by the brethren, mortifying the flesh and abasing the spirit.

Already in Tertullian's time this severity was becoming a painful strain on the Church; a time was coming when it became unbearable. Except for a few sporadic attacks on individuals there had been no persecutions since the death of Septimus Severus, thirty-eight years earlier. A whole generation had grown up in peace and apparent security, and the Church had flourished and expanded all over the Empire. But in A.D. 249 Decius appeared on the scenes.

Decius, one of the most virtuous of the Emperors—"in life and death worthy to be ranked with the Romans of old time"— was a convinced enemy of Christianity. He regarded it as a dangerous and disgusting superstition, which must at all costs be stamped out. He began by attacking the bishops. The Patriarchs of Antioch and Jerusalem were thrown into prison, where they shortly succumbed to their sufferings. Origen, though not a bishop, was so eminent a figure that he too was imprisoned and tortured. Fabian was executed in January 250. Dionysius of Alexandria, Gregory Thaumaturgus and Cyprian of Carthage decided that their right course was to fly and conceal themselves till the storm had passed. But the storm increased in intensity, and soon Christians everywhere were sought out and offered the choice between recanting and death by torture. It at once became apparent that the long peace had brought into the fold many who were Christians only in name, and many whose faith was not strong enough to withstand to the end. There was, it is true, no lack of staunch believers who held out in the face of all the enemy could do. Among these we may mention Celerinus, whose story can be pieced together from the contemporary letters of Cyprian.

Celerinus was a Carthaginian resident at Rome. He and several others were seized at the same time as Fabian, and put to the torture, apparently in the presence of Decius himself. He remained firm and was thrown into prison, where for several months the tortures were continued—he was in the stocks without food and water for nineteen days—but nothing moved him. He was eventually released, and returning to Carthage presented himself to Cyprian, whom he sought out in his hiding place. Cyprian describes him as scarred and broken in health by his sufferings, having been brought so near to death that he lived only "through a kind of resurrection". Yet he was "lowly in ... peacefulness and tranquillity ... and fitted both for conflict and peace; praiseworthy in the former for strength, in the latter for modesty".

Celerinus came of a martyr family; his grandmother and two of his uncles had suffered in previous persecutions. But his sisters were not so devoted. Candida had offered sacrifice, Etecusa, actually on her way to the heathen altar, had paid money for an exemption from the test. The two young women were excommunicated. In sincere remorse for their weakness they devoted themselves to the care of sufferers from the persecution, and at one time had sixty-five of them whom they helped and tended.

The Church was now in a painful dilemma. According to the established custom none who had apostatised could be received back into communion; they must remain as penitents until death, trusting to find forgiveness from God. But the numbers of the lapsed were so enormous that to abide by this custom would have meant the disintegration of the Church. There was a rush of terrified people to the altars to save their lives by sacrifice. "Many," says Cyprian, "did not wait to be interrogated before they denied. Many were conquered before the battle, prostrated before the attack ... They ran to the market-place of their own accord." If they arrived at evening when the magistrate was leaving they begged him not to defer witnessing their sacrifice. There were, moreover, degrees of criminality. Small children—infants—were carried to the altars, incense pushed between their fingers and dropped on the flames. Were these helpless, innocent apostates to be excluded for ever from the Church? Then there were those who actually burnt incense—the Thurificati—and obtained from the magistrate a document testifying that they had done so. Sometimes a proxy in the shape of a heathen friend or slave performed the ceremony in the Christian's name, or the head of a family to save his wife and children might take on himself the guilt of apostasy. A certificate of exemption might be obtained by purchase, though these certificates can hardly have been obtained except by some private denial of the faith. About fifty years ago two such *libelli*, as the certificates were called, were found in the Fayoum of Egypt, written on papyrus leaves.

To the Commissioners of the sacrifices in the village of Philadelphia, from Aurelius Syrus and Pasbeius his brother, and Demetria and Sciapias our wives. Dwellers outside the gates, we were constant in ever sacrificing to the gods, and now in your presence, according to the precepts, we both poured libations and tasted of the victims, and we beseech you to attach your signature for us. May you ever prosper.
We, Aurelius Syrus and Pasbeius, have delivered this.
I, Isidorus, wrote for them, as unlettered.

Were all these to be lumped together as unpardonable sinners, kept till the day of their death, all the while, if they hoped for salvation, fasting and weeping in sackcloth and ashes, at the door of the church?
Meanwhile a new difficulty arose. Face to face with the Lapsed were the Martyrs, who died for their faith, and the Confessors, who like Celerinus suffered but escaped death.

These were the saviours of the faith, and men's gratitude and veneration for them knew no bounds. They were visited by crowds, who rushed to the prisons to supply the wants of the prisoners and to join them in prayer and communion. The enthusiasm they aroused reached extravagant heights, the blood they had shed seemed to have endued them with a more glorious priesthood, and the Lapsed, agonising in their sins and hopeless penance, turned to them for relief. The Martyrs were not loath to respond. At first their petitions were on a modest scale. Mappalicus, who suffered at Carthage, begged as he was dying for pardon for his mother; Celerinus, himself a confessor, implored that his two sisters, who since their sin had led a penitent and devotional life, might be received back into the Church. Whether these prayers were accepted is not known. In any case they rapidly increased in number, comprehensiveness and imperiousness. "Allow this man and his family to communicate," ran one appeal. The Confessor Paul desired that "Peace" should be given in his name to whoever asked for it. Finally, Lucian, a friend of Celerinus, "himself one of the confessors", says Cyprian, "earnest indeed in faith and robust in virtue, but little acquainted with the Lord's word", went so far as to send Cyprian an indulgence, in the name of "All Confessors" to "All the Lapsed" and desired him to communicate it to the other bishops. Presently some thousands of these indulgences were, it was thought, scattered broadcast over Africa.

The discipline of the Church, the authority of the bishops, was thus undermined. Too strict a discipline had led to the relaxation of all law. Cyprian was well aware of the danger in which the Church stood, and fought valiantly to restore order. He saw that the old, harsh treatment of penitents must be abandoned, but some rule, some order, must be preserved. Let the Lapsed wait till Peace was restored. Each claim could then be considered, the degree of the crime and the genuine penitence of the sinner could be taken into account, and the bishop could restore to the Church those who had earned a pardon. He wrote innumerable letters to other bishops, to presbyters, to confessors, urging patience and obedience. He described the fatal results of admitting to communion those who were unworthy.

"Learn what occurred when I myself was present and a witness," he writes. "Some parents who were escaping (from the persecution) left a little daughter in the care of a wet nurse. The nurse took the baby before the magistrates, who gave it bread dipped in wine, since it was too young to eat the sacrificial flesh." The mother returned and took back her infant, who being unable to speak could not describe what had happened. The mother, in complete ignorance, brought the child into church during a celebration of the Eucharist. "The infant became impatient of our prayers and supplications, and was at one time shaken with weeping and at another tossed about like a wave of the sea by the violent excitement of her mind. . . . When, however, the deacon began to offer the cup to those present . . . the little child, by the instinct of the divine majesty, compressed. its mouth, resisted with its lips, and refused the cup. Still the deacon persisted, and although against her efforts, forced on her some of the Sacrament. There followed sobbing and vomiting—for the Eucharist could not remain in a profane mouth and stomach."

This infant was too young to be personally to blame; but a woman of advanced years who "secretly crept in among us when we were sacrificing, received not food, but a sword for herself. As if she had taken some deadly poison . . . she began to be tortured. Her body stiffened in a convulsion; suffering the pangs, not of persecution but of her sin, she shivered, she trembled, she fell to the ground. Another woman when she tried with unworthy hands to open the box in which was the holy body of the Lord,[1] was deterred by fire rising from it from daring to touch it. Another, a man who was defiled

[1] It was customary for communicants to take home with them the sacred bread.

by sacrificing, when he dared to receive secretly the holy Eucharist, found he was holding in his hands[1] nothing but a cinder."

In Africa these disorders were caused by the undisciplined Lapsed, supported by many presbyters who were the personal enemies of Cyprian. In Rome difficulties were caused by those who instead of being too lax were too strict. After the death of Fabian, while the persecution was still at its height, no new bishop was elected, but towards the beginning of 251, Decius having left Rome to oppose a rival Augustus, the Christians began to consider the appointment of a new Pope. The suffrages of most of the presbyters were given to Cornelius; but his election was attacked by a body of men who were violently opposed to any relaxation of the old rule—no apostate was ever to be received back into the Church. This group was headed by Novatian. He and his followers proved quite irreconcilable, and eventually formed a schismatic body which continued to exist for over three hundred years.

Meantime Cyprian had left his hiding place and returned to Carthage. Peace had come, and in accordance with the views he had put out during the persecution, he set to work to deal individually with the problem of the Lapsed. Little by little order was restored to the Church. Cyprian's enemies faded away, he was supported by the other African bishops, and by 253 the matter was settled. It was decided that lapsed priests and bishops could never be restored to holy orders, but they, and "all who had continued so far steadfast in penance", were at once re-admitted to communion.

The Last Years of Cyprian

We are particularly well documented as to the years of Cyprian's episcopate, for he left a voluminous correspondence

---

[1] At this period the bread of Communion was put into the hands of the communicant.

of about eighty letters, extending over the years 249 to 258. He is the first of many of the fathers to have left a great body of letters—we may mention among later writers Basil the Great (329–379), the two Gregories, Jerome and Augustine. In our account of the question of the Lapsed we have drawn very largely on the earlier epistles. His later letters deal fully with the other struggle in which he was involved—the question of the rebaptism of heretics. As this is in reality a theological question we shall not enter into it, but merely mention that in this case the final decision of the Church was against Cyprian. Cyprian was of opinion that heretical baptism was no baptism at all, and those who wished to give up their heresy and join the Catholic Church must be rebaptised. He carried with him most of the bishops of the East; we find his teaching even in Wicliffe, who pronounced, "If a bishop or priest is in mortal sin he cannot ordain, give communion *or baptise*." This doctrine was opposed by the Pope Stephen, Dionysius of Alexandria, and was finally condemned by the whole Catholic Church. In this controversy, therefore, Cyprian in the end was defeated.

Without pursuing this question further there is one point in connection with baptism that may be of interest. A certain bishop Fidus wrote to the Council of Carthage, presided over by Cyprian, saying that infants should not be baptised till the eighth day—the law of ancient circumcision should be regarded. Cyprian, in the name of the council, replies, "You say that the appearance of an infant in the first days after its birth is not pure, so that anyone would shudder at kissing it;[1] we do not think that this ought to be alleged as any impediment to heavenly grace . . . nor should anyone shudder at kissing it in giving grace and making peace." He adds that a new-born infant comes fresh from God's creating hands, and when we kiss it we are embracing the handiwork of God. A hundred and sixty years later Augustine read this

[1] The kiss was part of the baptismal ritual.

letter to the Pelagians, as a defence of the doctrine of Infant Baptism.

Besides his religious and ecclesiastical duties the bishop at this time had to be the administrator of his community. In any emergency it was his duty to organise and control his flock. Two such emergencies arose during Cyprian's episcopate. The first of these was the great Berber raid into Numidia in A.D. 252. In this raid many towns were burnt and ravaged, men, women and children,[1] among them many hundred Christians, were carried away into slavery. The raids continued sporadically till the fifth century—in 409 we hear of them from Augustine. From the days of Cicero the Romans had looked upon the ransoming of captives as a commendable act of charity. Cyprian organised this charity among his Christian flock. He collected a sum of about eight hundred pounds for the benefit of the victims, chiefly from poor contributors, and sent it to the bishop of Numidia with a list of the subscribers and a promise of more if further help was required.

The other disaster, even more terrible, was the plague. For twenty years this frightful disease ravaged the whole Roman Empire; it reached Carthage in A.D. 252, the same year as the Berber raid. Against such epidemics the Romans had no defence. The Emperors had only two weapons against it— repeated edicts for universal sacrifice, and the issue from the imperial mints of coins dedicated to "Healthful Apollo". No sanitary methods were adopted, people fled in terror from the sick, the dying were abandoned in the streets, and every sense of decency and restraint collapsed. The bishops alone made some attempt to bring order to the demoralised community; Gregory in Pontus, Dionysius in Alexandria, were active in organising some sort of health service among the Christians. Cyprian was naturally not behindhand in his efforts. He summoned his flock together and enjoined on them the duty of prayer and labour on behalf of their fellow-citizens. He had

---

[1] *V.* Commodian, p. 199.

ready a scheme for nursing the sick and burying the dead, and it is to be noted that no discrimination on religious grounds was to be made. His proposals were enthusiastically accepted, money was raised and willing workers brought together. But such devotion met with no recognition, no gratitude from the heathen. The old complaint, that all misfortunes were due to the impiety of those who would not worship the Roman deities, increased to frenzy, and the cry "The Christians to the lions!" was heard everywhere, with mounting fury.

Cyprian answers the accusation in a treatise that takes the form of a letter *To Demetrianus*, a persecuting magistrate. He admits that everything has gone to the bad, but this is not because of the Christians—it is because the world itself is dying of old age. Old men might as well blame the Christians because they are not as vigorous as they were and that their faculties—sight, hearing, agility—are not as keen as in youth.

"In the winter there is not such an abundance of showers for nourishing the seeds; in the summer the sun has not so much heat for cherishing the harvest; in the spring the cornfields are not so smiling; nor is the autumn so fruitful in leafy products. Marble is dug out in smaller quantities from the bowels of the weary mountains; the impoverished veins of gold and silver day by day approach exhaustion. The husbandman is failing in the fields, the sailor on the sea, the soldier in the camp, innocence in the market place, justice in the law court, concord in friendship, skill in the arts, discipline in morals. Do you think the substance of a thing that is growing old retains the strength that made it flourish when young and vigorous? Whatever is tending towards decay must necessarily be weakened as its end rapidly approaches. Thus the sun, when setting, darts forth his rays with a less bright and fiery splendour. Thus, in her last phase, the moon wanes with diminished horns. The tree, once green and fertile, as its branches dry up, presently becomes deformed in a barren old age; and the fountain which used to gush out copiously from overflowing channels, as old age causes it to fail, barely trickles down in a few scanty drops. All this is caused, not by the guilt of the Christians, but by the approaching end of the world."

Even the Christians themselves were shaken by this terrible visitation. Some protested that death from the plague robbed them of the martyr's crown, some, unnerved by their common suffering, felt unable to face the horrors of the ever-threatening persecution. Others, weaker still, were shaken in their faith. How was it possible that God should permit the hideous disease to attack his faithful servants and make no difference between them and the wicked heathen? To this Cyprian made the answer of common sense.

"It disturbs some," he writes, "that this mortality is common to us and to others; and yet what is there in this world that is not common to us with others so long as this flesh of ours still remains? . . . Thus when the earth is barren and the harvest is unproductive, famine makes no distinction. When the enemy invades a country and seizes a town, captivity at once desolates all the inhabitants. When the clouds withhold their rain, drought is the same to everyone. When the ship strikes a jagged rock, all who are aboard suffer shipwreck. Ophthalmia, fever, weakness, is common to us all so long as this common flesh of ours is borne by us in the world."

To those who longed for martyrdom he points out that if the hour of trial had come they might not have stood firm, and that if they are indeed faithful their intention is known to God and will be rewarded by him. The fear of death is unworthy of a Christian, who should trust to God's promises, and rejoice at being removed from the miseries of this life to a world of eternal salvation.

"One of our colleagues, a priest fearing the approach of death, prayed for a respite. As he prayed he saw beside him a youth, venerable in honour and majesty, lofty in stature and shining of aspect, whose glory could hardly be borne to the sight except of one about to die. In a tone of indignation he rebuked him, saying, 'You fear to suffer; you fear to depart; what shall I do to you?' " This angelic monition, says Cyprian, was meant for us—it could be of no use to one who was himself already on the eve of departure. Death is a cause of rejoicing rather than dread. "Who that has been living in foreign lands would not hasten to return to his own country? Who that is sailing homewards would not eagerly desire a prosperous wind that he might the sooner embrace his dear ones? We regard paradise as our country . . . why do we not hasten and run . . . that we may greet our parents? A dense crowd of parents, brothers, children, is awaiting us, longing for us, already assured of their own safety and still anxious for our salvation. How lofty and perpetual a happiness shall we find in the heavenly kingdom! There are the glorious company of the apostles, the host of rejoicing prophets, the innumerable multitude of martyrs . . . the triumphant virgins . . . and the merciful men who have kept the Lord's precepts. . . . To these, beloved brethren, let us hasten with an eager desire; let us crave to be quickly with them and quickly to come to Christ."

With such cares—confuting heathens and heretics, strengthening the Church, organising charitable labours, teaching and admonishing his flock—Cyprian's busy life was fully occupied. Five years after the Berber raid and the outbreak of the plague, the end came in sight. The Emperor Valerian, who for two years had maintained a tolerant and even friendly attitude towards the Christians, changed his policy and decided that they were a menace to the solidarity of the Empire, already threatened with enemies without and disease within. He determined to put an end to the "illicit religion", which with its separate organisation, its refusal to worship the Emperor, and its rapid increase in numbers, seemed to endanger the unity of the Empire. Valerian at first thought he could achieve his object by removing the Christian leaders and closing the cemeteries, their places of assembly and worship. Many bishops, among them Dionysius of Alexandria, were sent into exile; Cyprian did not escape. In A.D. 257 he was arrested, and ordered to leave Carthage for the remote village of Cucusus. Nine years before, during the persecution of Decius, Cyprian had fled in order to continue to help and supervise his flock from a distance. His enemies had accused him of cowardice; that it was not so he proved by his action under Valerian. His friends begged him to escape and offered him every help in their power. But Cyprian refused all such entreaties—he knew the time for him to give his last testimony had arrived. On the first night of his arrival at Cucusus he had a dream or vision which he described to his deacon Pontius who afterwards wrote his biography.

"That night," he said, "before I was fully asleep, there appeared before me a young man of superhuman height. He seemed to lead me up to the Praetorium and I seemed to be standing at the Tribunal before the Proconsul. He looked up at me and immediately began to write in his tablets—what it was I did not know, for he had not asked me the usual questions. But the young man, who was standing behind him, read attentively what he had written down. As he could not speak to me from where he was, he made gestures to indicate what was on the tablets. He opened his hand, and holding it flat like the blade of a sword imitated the stroke given in an ordinary execution. He expressed what he wished me to understand as clearly as if he had spoken. I understood it was the death sentence. I began to beg and entreat that he would grant me just one day's respite so that I could arrange my affairs. After I had entreated him for some time the Proconsul made a further note on his tablets. I perceived from the calmness of his expression that my judge considered my request a reasonable one. And besides, the youth who had signalled to me before that I was to die, now, by secretly nodding his head and twisting his fingers one behind another, conveyed to me that the reprieve I had asked for was granted. Though the sentence had not been actually read I woke up rejoicing that I had received a reprieve. And yet the uncertainty of the interpretation caused me to tremble with such dread that my heart was still throbbing with the excess of my agitation."

The "one day" of the dream turned out to be a year, for a year later to the very day the dream came true. Cyprian spent this year of delay in doing what he could for his fellow sufferers. Many bishops were imprisoned, sent to the mines, half starved, beaten with cudgels; Cyprian supported them with money and letters of comfort and sympathy; they answered gratefully, telling him they were strengthened by his messages and the example of his fortitude in suffering.

Valerian spent the year in a different mood. His scheme of breaking the Church by separating it from its leaders had failed completely. A heavier blow must be struck. All bishops, presbyters and deacons were to be immediately executed. Lay Christians were to forfeit their rank and their property; matrons to be banished, others to be reduced to slavery. The persecution, though perhaps more widespread than that of Decius, was apparently not quite so cruel. In any case there were this time but few Lapsed. The Church was shaken outwardly, but inwardly remained firm.

The trial and death of Cyprian are very fully described in his life by Pontius, an eye-witness, and in the official Proconsular Acts. He was brought before the Proconsul, who questioned him briefly as to his beliefs. Cyprian refused to sacrifice to the Emperor, and on the Proconsul begging him to reconsider, replied, "Do what you are charged to do. The matter is so simple that there is nothing to consider." The Proconsul then read aloud the sentence of death, and Cyprian was 'led out to an amphitheatre in the grounds. A vast crowd of sympathisers followed, many of them calling out, "Let us be beheaded along with him." When they reached the place of execution Cyprian removed his outer clothing and tied a handkerchief over his eyes. The executioner—perhaps a secret sympathiser, or perhaps unnerved by the shouts of the spectators—could hardly hold his weapon, and dropped his trembling hand. The centurion in command took his sword, and with one blow—"the power granted from above", says Pontius—severed the saint's head from his body.

Novatian

We have already said something concerning Novatian in a previous chapter. He deserves, however, fuller treatment, both as a writer and the leader of an important sect.

During the persecution of Decius, A.D. 250, both the Church of Rome and the Church of Carthage were deprived of their bishops—Rome by the martyrdom of Fabian, Carthage by the withdrawal of Cyprian to a place of safety. The clergy of Rome thereupon took it upon themselves to write to the clergy of Carthage in terms at once impertinent and ungrammatical. They compared Fabian, the good shepherd who died for his sheep, to Cyprian, the hireling, who fled at the approach of the wolf. They warned the Carthaginian clergy not to neglect their duties; they themselves, they went on, "by the blessing of God have done and still do all that we should, though it entails anxiety and worldly risk, having before our eyes rather the fear of God and eternal suffering than the fear of men and a short-lived discomfort". They even saw fit to urge the Carthaginians not to neglect the widows and orphans, and to bury the martyrs. This extraordinary composition was of course handed over to Cyprian, who was amazed and indignant at its contents. He wrote immediately to Rome, in polite but crushing terms. "I have read a letter with neither address nor signature. The writing, the matter and even the paper on

which it is written made me think it could not be genuine. . . .
I therefore return it to you that you may see if it is really the
letter sent by you."

What the Roman clergy thought of all this we do not know,
but they soon adopted a different tone and a different scribe.
Novatian was entrusted with their further correspondence
and he showed himself an intelligent man and a good Latinist.
In the difficult question of the treatment of the Lapsed he ranged
himself on the side of Cyprian and agreed with him that a
lenient treatment should be accorded them.

This pleasant state of affairs was not, however, of long
duration. The enemies of Cyprian in Carthage continued
their intrigues against him. Among them was a certain
Novatus, described as "greedy of novelty, raging with the
rapacity of an insatiable avarice, inflated with the arrogance
and stupidity of swelling pride. He had always had a bad
reputation among the bishops of Africa, had always been condemned by all the priests as a heretic and a perfidious man,
always inquisitive and treacherous. He flatters that he may
deceive. . . . He is a torch and a flame to blow up the fires of
sedition, a whirlwind and tempest to make shipwreck of the
faith, the foe of quiet, the adversary of tranquillity, the enemy
of peace". Charges of specific crimes were brought against
him by Cyprian. "Orphans despoiled by him, widows
defrauded, moneys of the Church withheld, demand the
severest penalties. His father also died of hunger in the street
and he did not even bury him. He kicked his wife in the womb
when she was pregnant, brought on a miscarriage and caused
the death of his unborn son." He was about to be brought
before the congregation to answer for his misdemeanours,
when by an abrupt change of front he managed to turn from
accused into accuser.

At the end of the persecution of Decius the Roman clergy
began to think of electing a new Pope. Novatus saw his
opportunity. He rushed across to Rome, and got into touch

with Novatian. What arts, what arguments he used we do not know, but Novatian was turned completely round. From being in accord with Cyprian he became a violent antagonist; from being a supporter of a reasonable mildness, he became a fanatical puritan. No apostate was ever to be forgiven. Let him do penance to the end of his days, the doors of the Church must be bolted and barred against him for ever.

He and Novatus now devoted themselves to intrigue. It seemed probable that Cornelius, a man of moderate views, would be elected to the vacant bishopric, as in spite of their efforts he actually was, A.D. 251. They did not, however, despair. Novatus hurried off on a tour of Italy and brought back with him three bishops, "rough and very simple men". Their doings when they arrived in Rome were described by Cornelius. "As they were too simple . . . for the unscrupulous devices of the wicked, they were shut up by certain disorderly men like Novatian, and at the tenth hour, when they were drunk and sick with the after effects, he forcibly compelled them to ordain him bishop by a counterfeit and inoperative laying on of hands." Novatian had become an Anti-Pope.

The question now arose as to how many of the faithful he could detach from the true Church. Several Roman confessors, recently released from prison, at first joined his party; but most of them soon repented and returned to communion with Cornelius. Novatian wrote formal letters to Cyprian, Dionysius of Alexandria and Fabius of Antioch, announcing his elevation and claiming their allegiance. Cyprian waited to hear from Rome and then wrote to Cornelius officially recognising him. Dionysius wrote mildly to Novatian telling him he was in the wrong and calling upon him to return to the Church. Fabius of Antioch was for a while led astray, but shortly afterwards the cause of Novatian was given up in Antioch too.

Cornelius, in his visitation, brought up the old story of Novatian's irregular ordination. The illness during which he received baptism was caused by the efforts of the exorcists to expel Satan who had possessed him for a long time. It was but a *clinical* baptism, and was never completed by confirmation. He shut himself up in a cell and refused to leave it when exhorted by the deacons to come to the help of the brethren who needed help, declaring that he did not wish to be a presbyter—he was enamoured of another philosophy. But the worst of all his offences was that in giving Communion to his disciples he held both the hands of the communicant in his and would not let him taste till he had sworn never to return to Cornelius.

Cornelius soon summoned a synod of sixty bishops to meet at Rome. They received letters from Carthage setting forth the principles on which the Lapsed were to be restored to the Church and condemning Novatian and his teaching. The Roman bishops concurred, and Novatian and his followers were formally expelled from the Church.

Novatianism did not spread much, though it had a fairly long life. It found a home in Carthage and was accepted by the Bishop of Arles in Gaul. It lingered in parts of the East and did not finally disappear till the end of the fifth century.

Whatever his faults Novatian was an eloquent and copious writer. Jerome mentions many of his writings, but only two have come down to us—the *Treatise on the Trinity*, and the one on *Jewish Foods*. An example from each of them may be given, though a translation will hardly do him justice.

Of the Trinity. "The Founder of all things, God Almighty . . . made the sky, poised above in its lofty height, the solid earth laid out beneath, the seas flowing freely in every direction; and He furnished all these, in full abundance and order, with their peculiar and appropriate characteristics. In the firmament of heaven He set the sun, aroused at each day's dawn to give light with his beams; the brilliant sphere of the moon, waxing to fullness with her monthly phases, to relieve the gloom of night; and the glittering stars shining with different degrees of intensity. It is by His will that they run their courses according to the laws of their orbits, to mark for mankind days, months, years and seasons. .... On the earth, too, He reared the mountains with their towering crests, hollowed out the deep valleys, levelled the plains and appointed the different species of animals to supply the various needs of man. He hardened the stout timber of the forests . . . called forth the fruits of the earth for food, unlocked the mouths of gushing springs and poured them forth to swell the gliding rivers."

Of Jewish Foods. Novatian on this subject adopts the same line of argument as Barnabas.[1] The Law is to be understood in a figurative sense—do not eat swine's flesh means do not behave like a pig. He adds, however, some details of his own.

"The only food for the first men was fruit and the produce of trees. Afterwards, man's sin transferred his need from the fruit trees to the produce of the earth, when the very attitude of his body showed the condition of his conscience. For though innocence raised men up towards the heavens to pluck their fruit from the trees so long as they had a good conscience, yet sin . . . bent men down to the earth . . . to gather its grain.

"Those animals are clean that chew the cud and divide the hoof; those are unclean that do neither the one nor the other. . . . In the animals it is the characters and acts and wills that are depicted: They are clean if they chew the cud; that is, if they ever have in their mouth as food the divine precepts. They divide the hoof, if with the firm step of innocence they tread the ways of righteousness. . . . For those creatures which divide the foot into two hoofs always walk with vigour; the tendency to slip with one part of the hoof being counteracted by the firmness of the other, and so retained in the substantial footstep."

The Law, he goes on, has now been abrogated for Christians —for them there is no distinction between clean and unclean

[1] *V.* p. 217.

animals. This of course does not allow luxurious and intemperate feeding—we should be moderate in all things. "There are however some who, although they claim the name of Christians, afford instances and teachings of intemperance. Their vices have come to such a pitch that they will drink in the early morning while fasting, for they do not think it Christian to drink after eating; the wine must be poured into their empty and unoccupied veins directly they wake from sleep—in fact they seem to have less relish for what they drink if food be mingled with the wine. Here you may see a new fashion—still fasting and already drunk, they do not run to the tavern, but carry about the tavern with them, and if they offer a salute, give not a kiss but drink a toast. What can they do after meat whom meat finds intoxicated? In what kind of state does the sun at his setting leave them, when at his rising he already sees them stupefied with wine?"

Commodianus

A few words may be said concerning this writer of wretched doggerel. He wrote towards A.D. 250, and thus is roughly speaking a contemporary of Cyprian and Novatian, to whose controversy about the Lapsed he seems to make an obscure reference. He writes in what purports to be hexameters, but his lines are based on accent and not on quantity. This, perhaps the first sign of Latin's metamorphosis into Romance, is of interest to the philologist—but for any other reason he is hardly worth more than a glance.

His two extant works are *Carmina Apologeticum*, described by a modern author as "a shrill Apocalypse", and the *Instructiones*, a series of discrete stanzas dealing with elementary Christian teaching and in the form of acrostics—the first letter of each line gives the name of the strophe.

Three examples will amply suffice. First, a description of exomologesis.

199

Thou art a penitent; turn not away
From Mother Church; morning and evening pray.
Confess thy fault; it shall not be in vain.
Walk cautiously and do not sin again.
Thy hair and beard rub on the dusty ground
And let thine eyes in tears of grief be drowned.
Call constantly for aid from God in heaven;
It may be at the last thou'lt be forgiven.

Perhaps on the question of Novatianism:

Ye faithful, do not hate your brother men.
You say you are a martyr; well, what then?
Even in a martyr hatred is a sin,
A martyr's crown no man who hates can win.
Hard-hearted man! sinning 'gainst things divine
And against man, a double sin is thine.
In baptism thou wast washed clean from stain:
Think not to be baptised and cleansed again.

One result of the Berber raid:

The enemy is here in sudden spate,
Flooding the land in violence and hate.
Even infants he has seized with cruel might—
They had no time to flee, no strength to fight.
Reproach them not, though they are captive seen;
Yet to excuse them quite I do not mean.
Maybe they suffer for their parents' sin
And for that cause God would not take them in.

The Wonderworker

Gregory, Bishop of Neo-Caesarea in Pontus from about
A.D. 250 to A.D. 265, is commonly called Thaumaturge or

Wonderworker, partly to distinguish him from the many other Gregories of the Church, partly to denote his powers as a performer of miracles. He was born in Neo-Caesarea of heathen parents, and in his youth studied Roman law. It was in pursuit of these studies that he went with his brother Athenodorus to Berytus in Syria, at that time the most important centre of legal learning. While there the brothers heard that the great Origen was staying nearby at Caesarea, and going to visit him soon fell under his charm. They abandoned law and devoted themselves to philosophy under Origen's instruction. When Gregory was leaving Caesarea he pronounced a panygyric on Origen, in which he gives a very interesting account of his methods of teaching.

The usual basis of advanced education at this period was rhetoric, and rhetoric divorced from any practical application. The pupils were taught to deliver speeches in a set form that never varied; the subject matter of their speeches was carefully divorced from real life and dealt with events of the past or fantastic imaginary situations—Agamemnon argues whether he should sacrifice Iphigenia, a man accuses his wife of adultery because a rich merchant had made her his heir as a tribute to her virtue. Origen would have none of this empty and pointless oratory, but inculcated logical thought and expression. "Our minds," says Gregory, "were trained . . . in a rational manner, not according to the judgements of illustrious rhetoricians, for theirs is a discipline of little value and no necessity." Besides logic he instructed his pupils in natural science, geometry, astronomy and ethics. His teaching of ethics was indeed unusual. "Not in mere words only did this teacher go over the truths concerning the virtues with us. He incited us much more to the practice of virtue, and stimulated us by what he did more than by the doctrines he taught."

His method of teaching was equally original. "He put us to the question, and made propositions to us, and listened to our replies. And whenever he detected anything in us not wholly fruitless and profitless he set about clearing the soil, turning it up and irrigating it . . . and brought his whole skill and care to bear on us, and wrought upon our mind." "Whenever he saw us getting restive under him, like so many unbroken horses, and springing out of the course and galloping about at random . . . with a strange kind of persuasiveness and constraint he reduced us to a state of quietude by his discourse, which acted like a bridle in our mouth." Gregory says that this was at first unpleasant, for they were not accustomed to such methods. But Origen's charm was too much for them. "He was possessed of a rare combination of a certain sweet grace and persuasiveness along with a strange power of control." "Moreover the stimulus of friendship was also brought to bear on us . . . the argument of a kind and affectionate disposition which showed itself benignantly in his words when he spoke to us and associated with us . . . 'and the soul of Jonathan was knit with David '."

It is not surprising that this remarkable teacher won his pupils over to Christianity; both Gregory and Anthenodorus were persuaded to abandon heathenism, and adopt the new religion. When they had left Caesarea, after a stay of five years, Origen wrote to Gregory to persuade him to become a presbyter. But Gregory was not yet ready for this step, and retired into a secluded spot to think matters out. While he was thus in retreat, Phaedimus, the bishop of Amasea in Pontus, wished to make him bishop of Neo-Caesarea, and as he could not discover his whereabouts he ordained him in his absence. When Gregory heard of this unprecedented action he gave way, reappeared at Neo-Caesarea, and was properly consecrated with all due formality.

The years of Gregory's episcopate proved the good judgement of Origen and Phaedimus. We are told that when he took over his see there were only seventeen Christians in the district; when he died there were only seventeen heathens. There are perhaps some indications that his converts were a little uncertain. During the Decian persecution he thought it wise to withdraw into the wilderness, taking his flock with him. Though doubtless their life there was hard, they escaped both martyrdom and the danger of apostatising which overcame so many Christian communities. Gregory's flock encountered another test, from which they could not escape. In A.D. 260 barbarian invaders from the north overwhelmed Pontus and for eight years ravaged the district. When they had withdrawn it was necessary to enquire into the conduct of the inhabitants during the occupation. In the so-called *Canonical Epistle* Gregory runs through the various misdemeanours of which his flock had been guilty and decides on the treatment of the offenders. They have eaten "barbarian meats"—but that is "no burden to us", as these meats had not been sacrificed to idols. The chaste women who were raped by their conquerors are blameless——they could not help themselves. But those who before were leading unchaste lives are "evidently objects of suspicion, also in the time of captivity". Some people took the opportunity of the disorders to seize other men's property—they must be excluded from the Church. It is no excuse to say they merely found the property, which had been abandoned by the owner who was in flight. Some, forgetting they were Christians, joined the barbarians, put to death their own countrymen and acted as guides to the enemy. Some are to this day "at such a pitch of cruelty and inhumanity as to be detaining by force certain captives who had made their escape." All such persons are "impious men, who know not the very name of the Lord". Among those who did not fall away there are a number who seem to think they are entitled to some form of recognition. Gregory deals sharply with such pretensions. "They who keep the commandment ought to keep it without any sordid covetousness, demanding neither recompense nor reward, nor fee nor anything else that bears the name of acknowledgement."

The last event of Gregory's life that we hear of is his presence at the Synod of Antioch (A.D. 265), at which the case of Paul of Samosata was heard.[1] He seems to have died shortly after-wards.

From Gregory's account of his education with its bias to-wards logic and science, and from the eminently practical nature of his management of his episcopate, he would seem the last person in the world to be hailed as a Wonderworker. His extant writings are quite matter of fact. How the tradition arose is mysterious, but that it was widespread and persistent is undeniable. About a hundred years after his death Gregory of Nyssa (335–395) wrote a panegyric on him, which consists of a long series of marvellous tales. Now Gregory of Nyssa was a native of Pontus, and his grandmother Macrina may have been one of the Wonderworker's converts. It has been suggested that Gregory of Nyssa was apt to be too credulous, and wove his account from the stories current in the countryside and the old wives' tales related by his grandmother. "This," says Cardinal Newman, "is not respectful either to St. Macrina or to St. Gregory Thaumaturgus, to say nothing of the treatment of St. Gregory Nyssen; plainly it can mean no-thing else but that St. Gregory did no miracles, and that it is weak, nay heathenish, to believe he did." Without adopting either an attitude of weak, heathenish credulity, or of dis-respect towards St. Macrina, St. Gregory Thaumaturge or St. Gregory of Nyssa, let us see what these wonders were.

At the time of his consecration Gregory received a special revelation. St. John the Evangelist appeared to him by the request of the Virgin Mary, mother of God, and delivered to him a Declaration of Faith. The declaration is extant and bears witness to the doctrine of the Trinity—but some modern authorities assert that it is a forgery of the fourth century, written, it is to be supposed, to substantiate the story of its revelation.

Of course there are many accounts of miraculous cures and exorcisms. Sometimes, Socrates the historian (*fl.* 458) says,

[1] *V.* p. 212.

the exorcisms were performed by letter. His first great miracle was performed at the beginning of his episcopate, just as he was entering his diocese. He was on his way, with a group of friends, when they were overtaken by night and rain. Opportunely they came across a heathen temple, famous for its oracles, and in this building they took refuge. As they entered, Gregory, being aware that it was a haunt of Satan, made the sign of the cross, and called upon the name of the Lord. To make their stay in this ill-omened edifice less hazardous, he spent the night in prayer, joining with his companions in chanting the psalms. At daybreak they went on their way, but they had not gone far before the priest of the temple coming in pursuit of them called to them to stop. He threatened to bring them before the magistrates; for, he said, the spirit which spoke through the oracle had been driven out by their incantations and was unable to return. Whether from fear of legal proceedings or out of charity to the agitated priest, Gregory tore a leaf out of his note-book and wrote on it, "Satan, you may enter." The priest hurried off with the permit, but before long returned. He had been amazed to find that the Christian had as much power to re-admit the oracular spirit as to expel it, and he begged for more information about the Deity which had such surprising powers. Gregory explained the mystery of the Incarnation, but the priest found this hard to swallow, and asked to be shown a corroborating miracle. Gregory immediately caused an enormous stone to move and the priest was instantly converted. And not the priest only. All the citizens of the adjacent town came out to meet him, and on the first day of his preaching were converted in sufficient numbers to form a church and build a place for Christian worship.

Such was the excellent initiation of the Thaumaturge to his diocese. His powers were speedily recognised and he was often called upon to display them. Two brothers were disputing over the division of their father's estate, which they had inherited. The estate included a large lake, and Gregory was asked to arbitrate between them. It seemed impossible to come to an agreement which would satisfy both the claimants, and they were preparing to settle the question by force of arms. The night before the proposed battle Gregory spent in prayer by the lake-side. Before morning the waters had dried up and a fertile plain was exposed to view which could easily enough be divided. Gregory of Nyssa says he had seen the spot, which in his day was covered with woods, farm land and dwelling houses. Gregory Thaumaturge seemed to have special power over water. The river Lycus, a large and turbulent stream, from time to time burst out through its embankments and caused disastrous floods. The inhabitants of the district, who were heathens, were nevertheless believers in Gregory's marvellous powers, and appealed to him for help. Gregory immediately set out on foot for the flooded district, a journey of perhaps a hundred miles. On reaching the spot where the embankment was broken through he planted his staff in the ground and returned home. The staff put forth buds and sprouted into a tree, and from that time the river Lycus never dared to break through the bounds fixed for it by the holy man's staff.

The last miracle of St. Gregory that we shall relate may perhaps have some doubt cast upon it by the fact that it is variously attributed to two other holy men—by Sozomen to St. Epiphanius and by Theodoret of Cyrrha to St. James of Assyria. As the saint was travelling by road he met two Jews who plotted to deceive him. One of them fell down as if dead; the other, bursting into a lament, begged an alms to buy a shroud for his friend. The holy man took off his cloak, laid it on the supposed corpse, and went his way. When he was out of sight the lamenting swindler called on the other to get up. But there was no reply; the ruffian who had feigned death was dead indeed. There are two different ends to the story. In one the living beggar pursues the saint and persuades him to restore his companion to life. In the other the saint remains obdurate, and the cheat is punished for his duplicity. Whichever version we adopt the story is no doubt full of edification.

Dionysius of Alexandria

We have already made some mention of Dionysius, commonly known as the Great. He was a pupil of Origen's, and like him head of the Alexandrian school. In 247 he became bishop of Alexandria, a post he held till his death in 267. The years of his episcopate were stormy; he passed through two great persecutions, a civil war, and the plague, which raged all over the Empire. He describes many of his adventures in letters quoted by Eusebius in his *Ecclesiastical History*.

When the persecution of Decius broke out he decided, like Cyprian and many others, to conceal himself. At first he merely remained in his own house and Sabinus, the prefect, sent out an officer to apprehend him. It never occurred to this officer that he would simply be staying at home, "but he went around, searching everything, the roads, the rivers, the fields where he suspected I was hidden. . . . But after the fourth day God bade me depart; He miraculously made a way, and with some difficulty I and my servants and many of the brethren set out together". Towards sunset, however, they fell into the hands of the soldiers who were searching for them, and the whole party was taken to Taposiris, a town about thirty miles from Alexandria.

His son Timothy had been away from home when the party had set out; when he returned he found the house deserted and guarded by soldiers, and learnt of his father's arrest. "One of the country-folk met Timothy, fleeing and distraught, and enquired the reason of his haste, and he told him the truth." It so happened that the countryman was on his way to a marriage feast. He went in to the guests, who were intending to make a night of it and told them Timothy's tale.

"And they all, with one accord, as if by a preconcerted impulse, jumped up and came running at full speed. They burst in upon us, shouting, and the soldiers who were guarding us took to flight. The men came upon us, lying as we were on pallets without bedding. And I—God knows that at first I thought they were robbers intending to plunder us—stayed on the bed, naked, except for a linen shirt. The rest of my garments, that were lying by, I held out to them. But they bade me get up and go out with all speed."

When Dionysius realised that they were friends come to his rescue he seems to have felt he was being robbed of the martyr's glory and crown. "I cried out, begging and beseeching them to go away and leave us alone; and I asked them, if they wished to do me a kindness, to anticipate the soldiers and cut off my head themselves. And while I was thus shouting . . . they lifted me up forcibly. I let myself fall on the ground on my back, but they seized me by the arms and legs, and dragged me outside. Gaius, Faustus, Peter and Paul, my companions and witnesses of it all, followed me. They also lifted me up in their arms, and setting me on the bare back of a donkey led me away."

Dionysius and his friends remained hidden till the death of Decius ended the persecution, and then returned to Alexandria. The bishop had to deal with the same difficulties concerning the Lapsed as had perplexed Cyprian. His mild, conciliatory nature forbade him to follow the intransigent methods of Novatian. He at once gave orders that all who had lapsed and repented were to be given communion when dying, and in this connection he tells a curious tale.

"There was a certain Serapion among us, an old man and a believer. He lived blamelessly for a long time, but in the day of trial fell. This man often begged for absolution, but no one paid him any heed. For he had actually sacrificed. He fell sick and remained for three successive days speechless and unconscious. But on the fourth day he rallied a little and called his grandson to him. 'How long, my child,' he said, 'will you hold me back? Be quick, I implore you, and obtain my release. Fetch me one of the presbyters.' With these words he relapsed into unconsciousness. The boy ran off at once to fetch the presbyter, but did not reach his house till nightfall, and found him ill and unable to come." The presbyter, however, remembered the orders Dionysius had given that all penitents should be allowed to communicate when dying, gave the child a small piece of the Eucharist, and told him to soak it and drop it into his grandfather's mouth. "Back came the boy with it, and when he was near, before he had entered, Serapion revived again and said, 'Hast thou come, child? The presbyter, I know, could not come. Do quickly what he ordered, and let me depart.' The boy soaked the consecrated wafer and at the same time poured it into his mouth, and when he had swallowed a little he immediately gave up the ghost."

This story was part of a letter Dionysius wrote to Fabius of Antioch who had been led into undue severity by the persuasions of Novatian. Like Cyprian, the bishop of Alexandria recognised different degrees of sin among those who had lapsed, and though not weakly indulgent was always on the side of mercy.

In 254 Valerian became Emperor. At first he was favourable to the Christians and Dionysius speaks in high terms of his tolerant attitude. But as we have seen, this did not last. Dionysius and several of his companions were brought before the prefect Æmilianus and told they must give up their religion. On their all refusing they were banished to a place called Cephro, in the Libyan desert. Dionysius says he had never heard of the place and did not know in which direction he was to travel. He was ill, and asked for a few days respite; but this was not granted and, he says, "I departed with a good grace, and made no disturbance." Cephro turned out to be in an utterly heathen district, and at first the exiles were pursued and stoned. But after a little time some of the inhabitants were converted, and left their idols for the true God. But Æmilianus did not leave him in peace. He moved him to the district of Colluthion, which though nearer Alexandria, was wilder and rougher than Cephro. Dionysius was "vexed and exceedingly angry", for he thought it was a haunt of robbers and entirely heathen. He became reconciled to it, however, on finding that it was so near the city that his friends could come and spend the night with him, and a congregation could easily be collected.

The persecution began to abate and Dionysius returned to Alexandria. But though the Church was almost at peace the city was not. A violent civil war broke out which divided the city into two camps. The dividing line ran down the main street, and it was impossible to cross it, so that Dionysius was obliged to communicate with his flock by letter. The waters of the harbour were so full of slaughtered men that they were like the Red Sea. The river was sometimes drier than a water-less desert; "at another time it overflowed to such an extent that it submerged the whole neighbourhood, both the roads and the fields . . . and always its course is defiled with blood and murders and drownings. . . . How cleanse the water that cleanses all things? . . . Or when might the air, made foul by the vile exhalations on all sides, become pure? . . . Everywhere corpses are rotting. . . . Yet men marvel and are at a loss as to whence come the constant plagues, the various forms of death, the manifold and great human mortality."

And it is true enough that the plague descended on Alexandria with frightful violence. The same scenes were witnessed as in Carthage and Rome—the heathen abandoning their friends at the first signs of disease, casting out the dying into the roads, leaving the corpses to rot on the highway, while the Christians, "or the most, at all events", says Dionysius, had no thought of their own danger, but nursed the sick and buried the dead with unflagging devotion.

The plague was endemic in Alexandria for many years, but its first fury died away and men could breathe again.

In A.D. 260 Valerian was made prisoner by Sapor, King of the Persians. He was succeeded by his son, Gallienus, who was favourable to the Christians and restored their church property to them. Dionysius writes of his reign, in a sort of ecstasy, "The monarchy put aside its old age and cleansed itself from its former wickedness and now blossoms forth in fuller bloom, is seen and heard more widely and spreads abroad everywhere."

In this almost idyllic atmosphere Dionysius spent the last four years of his troubled life. He did not however sink down in indolence, but occupied himself with the duties of his diocese and literary labours. He carried on a voluminous correspondence, writing to the Pope Dionysius, his namesake, on theological questions, to a private enemy Germanus, who accused him of cowardice in flying from the Decian persecution, to Bishop Basilides, who consulted him on questions of Church order. He refuted and converted the heretic Korakion, after arguing with him uninterruptedly for four days. Among his numerous other writings he made a most interesting study of the Revelation of St. John the Divine. He did not question its canonicity but proved by an analysis of the language that it was certainly not written by the author of St. John's Gospel. He inclined to think it was composed by John the Elder, mentioned by Papias. This is a view that has been accepted by many modern scholars. Dionysius the Great, like Julius Africanus, may claim to be one of the first and most brilliant of the textual critics.

In his old age he had a reputation in the Church of unequalled sanctity and knowledge. As we shall see, he was invited by the bishops of Asia to preside over an important synod to be held at Antioch in A.D. 264. But he was old and failing; he could not, he said, make the journey; and before the year was out he was dead.

Zenobia and Paul of Samosata

Zenobia, Queen of Palmyra! From our childhood she has been a mysterious and romantic figure, a warrior queen who heroically and unsuccessfully defied the Roman Empire, and was carried to Rome to be shown as a prisoner in the triumph of the Emperor Aurelian. It will perhaps come as a surprise to learn that she was involved, if somewhat indirectly, in the struggles of the Church with an influential heretic, Paul of Samosata.

Palmyra, or as it is called in the Bible, Tadmor in the Wilderness, is situated some 100 miles to the north-east of Damascus. It lies now, a golden relic, ruined and abandoned in the golden sands of the desert. But in the early centuries of our era it was an important town, "a city," says Pliny, "famous for its situation, for the richness of its soil, and for its agreeable springs." It formed a buffer between the Roman and Persian empires, always involved in their perennial struggles. Though claimed by the Romans as a *colonia*, she retained enough independence to be an effective counterpoise between the two antagonistic powers. In 260 the Persian King Sapor inflicted a severe defeat on the Romans and made the Emperor Valerian prisoner. Odaenatus, at that time ruler of Palmyra, seized the opportunity to strengthen his own position. He obtained from the new Emperor, Gallienus, the title of King, and by inflicting a severe defeat on Sapor appeared to be promoting the interests of Rome. It was in reality the interests of Palmyra he was promoting. He did not stop at defeating the Persians, but extended his conquests over Armenia and the greater part of the Roman Orient. He would perhaps have made himself the independent ruler of these Eastern provinces had he not been assassinated, together with his eldest son, in 264. But this did not arrest the continued progress of Palmyra. The power fell into the hands of Zenobia, the widow of Odaenatus, who ruled in the name of her young son, Wahballath.

Zenobia was a remarkable woman. She was a celebrated beauty, and famous as a huntress and warrior. When, after her husband's death, she became head of the state, she continued Odaenatus's policy of expansion, and managed, without antagonising Rome, to seize the greater part of Asia Minor and make her son King of Egypt. Besides being an able politician she occupied herself with intellectual matters. She was familiar with Greek, Latin, and her native Syriac. She studied Plato and Homer, and had as one of her chief counsellors Longinus, the Athenian philosopher and critic and reputed author of the celebrated treatise *On the Sublime*. She was naturally interested in religion, and seems to have been inclined to some sort of syncretistic monotheism. She was supposed by many to have adopted the beliefs of the Jews, and though this is almost certainly untrue, she certainly was sympathetic towards them, and restored a Jewish synagogue in Egypt. She also showed friendly feelings towards the Christians, and one of her *protégés* was Paul of Samosata, the Bishop of Antioch.

All we know of Paul is from his bitterest enemies, the leaders of the orthodox church, and we know already that where the Christians differed in their theological tenets they invariably accused their opponents of every conceivable moral delinquency. No doubt they were sometimes right, but to what extent it is difficult to tell, as only the accusations are before us and Paul's defence of his character—if he made one—has vanished in oblivion.

From the one-sided account that remains to us we gather that Paul anticipated the politically ambitious prelates of a later age. Besides his bishopric he held an office in the civil government. He was a *ducenarius*, an official so called from the amount of his salary—about £1,600 a year—who was usually connected with the management and collection of taxes. Paul, we are

THE FATHERS WITHOUT THEOLOGY

told, preferred the title of *ducenarius* to that of Bishop. Apart from the handsome salary, the office was doubtless a lucrative one. His wealth was one of the proofs alleged by his opponents of his criminal activities. He had formerly been a poor man, and had certainly not inherited money from his father nor earned it by any trade or occupation. His wealth, they said, was the result of "lawless deeds, sacrilegious plunderings and extortions exacted from the brethren by threats". He was naturally much occupied by his secular affairs. He was seen, strutting about the market-place, reading and dictating letters as he walked in public, surrounded by a large bodyguard. He even set up in the church a private room in which to transact his business. His conduct of the church services was, as might be expected, even more scandalous. He erected a lofty throne for himself, gesticulated and stamped during his sermons, and encouraged his listeners to applaud, wave their handker-chiefs, shout and jump to their feet, as if they were in a theatre. Those who sat still and silent, behaving with the reverence becoming in God's house, he rebuked and insulted. It should, however, be observed that all Bishops had thrones from which they preached—the throne of St. James, the brother of Christ and head of the Church of Jerusalem, was long preserved and honoured. The applause and enthusiasm of the congregation was perhaps something new, but it soon became customary and widespread, and is mentioned, though certainly with disapproval, by Cyril of Jerusalem, St. John Chrysostom, and St. Augustine himself. But worse things than this took place in the cathedral of Antioch. He put a stop to the singing of the usual Psalms on the pretext that they were modern innova-tions. But it was an obvious pretext, for he introduced instead hymns sung by women in his own honour, even on Easter day, which would make one shudder to hear. The morals of this worldly prelate were just as scandalous. He was arrogant, boastful and tyrannical, for he terrified many into subjection, and won over others by winking at their offences, or even bribing them, so that no one dared to accuse him. Worst of all he kept with him "in luxury and surfeiting" two young and beautiful girls and encouraged others to do the like.

In spite of this openly reprehensible conduct Paul's enemies cannot conceal that he had a large following of enthusiastic admirers, both in Antioch itself and in the surrounding countryside. How are we to account for this, and also for the continued support he received from Zenobia? The reasons were undoubtedly partly political and partly theological. The district was divided in sympathy between the adherents of Rome and the adherents of Zenobia. So long as Paul showed an anti-Roman bias Zenobia would uphold him; so long as Zenobia upheld him Paul would be the enemy of Rome. Moreover their religious outlook was similar. Paul was so strong a monotheist that he belittled the position of Christ. He was accused of Judaising, often in the same passages where Zenobia is said to be a Jewess. "Wonder always comes upon me," says St. John Chrysostom, "at the madness of Paul of Samosata. Like the Jews, to gratify a certain woman, he dared to deny the pre-existence of Christ." "Zenobia was a Jewess," says Athanasius, "and a supporter of Paul of Samosata." The truth underlying these erroneous statements is most probably the inclination of both Zenobia and Paul towards a combination of philosophy and religion, a mixture of the Palmyran religion, Christianity and Greek rationalism. One of Paul's chief offences lay in his opposition to the allegorical method of interpreting scripture, then in almost universal use among the Fathers, and his love of dialectic and argument. In this he resembled a heretical sect which had flourished in Rome some time previously. The leader was Artemas, and Paul was said by his enemies to have revived his heresy. This was a truly shocking one. If anyone brought forward a text of scripture they examined it to see if it was logical. They studied the geometry of Euclid and admired Aristotle and the celebrated doctor, Galen. They even compared different copies of the

Scripture and found that they did not agree one with the other and were even inconsistent in themselves. They actually went so far as to make emendations, thus adding to the sin of using logic the worse one of textual criticism. "Thus on the pretence of their wicked and godless teaching they have fallen to the lowest destruction of perdition"; and of this body of detestable miscreants Paul of Samosata was the spiritual ally.

It is most probable that Paul's iniquitous life would have been winked at by the Church, but his heretical views and teaching were another matter. The scandal grew in intensity and in 264 the Bishops of Asia determined to take action. They agreed to meet in a Synod at Antioch, and invited Dionysius, the much-respected Bishop of Alexandria, to preside over their discussions. Dionysius, however, refused their invitation. He was, he said, too old and infirm to make the journey, and the bishops chose as their president Firmilian, Bishop of Cappadocia. The Synod met and summoned Paul to attend. But Paul was not so easily convicted of heresy. He was skilful and wily in argument, he slipped from one position to another, and he continued to maintain that he held the true apostolic doctrine. It was only after many long and wearisome sessions that he admitted he might have erred on some points. But even then the course of the bishops was not easy. Their standing in Antioch was dubious. By what right could they interfere in the concerns of an independent diocese? Firmilian, who had already maintained that each bishop was responsible only to his own flock, and had written an indignant letter to the Bishop of Rome protesting against his interfering in the affairs of Asia, felt uneasy as to the Synod's action. Paul was eventually persuaded to promise that he would conform to the orthodox beliefs, and the Synod reluctantly dispersed.

The uncomfortable mood in which the bishops separated was fully justified. Paul made no change in his teaching or his way of life. Supported by Zenobia, admired and upheld by a large body of Antiochians, he cared nothing for the protests of the bishops, who from his point of view were mere outsiders. For four years the orthodox bishops raged impotently. Dionysius of Alexandria died, Firmilian was in bad health. Most of the leaders of the first Synod had, one way or another, disappeared from the scene, when at last in 268 another Synod was summoned to meet at Antioch. On his way to join it Firmilian died at Tarsus, so that the new Synod consisted of a new set of accusers. Among them was a certain Malchion, a somewhat enigmatical figure. He was a presbyter of the church and at the same time a teacher of rhetoric in the heathen school of the Greeks. His skill in controversy was well known and he was selected by the Synod to conduct the examination of Paul. He had the wisdom to engage a shorthand writer, who made a complete verbatim report of the discussion, a report which was preserved till the fifth century, though only fragments are now extant. They are enough however to show how the slippery bishop was finally outmanoeuvred by the subtle priest. He was pressed, nailed down, forced into absurd or contradictory statements, and finally convicted, without a shadow of doubt, of the worst form of heresy. The Synod retired in triumph. They composed and circulated throughout the Church a letter in which they exposed the moral and theological crimes of which Paul was guilty, and announced that they had condemned, excommunicated and deposed him, and appointed another, Domnus, bishop of Antioch in his stead.

It might be thought that the Synodal letter spelt the final ruin of the peccant bishop. Not at all. Paul paid not the slightest attention to the excommunication and deposition he had incurred. Strong in the protection of Zenobia and the fidelity of the Christians of Antioch, he remained in possession of the Cathedral and Church buildings, continued to live in the bishop's palace, and pursued his teaching and way of life quite undisturbed by the fulminations of his enemies. The orthodox could now do no more. They had shot their bolt, and all they had

to show for their nominal success was a bishop functioning
in a small and wretched building, with an attenuated and
despicable congregation. Domnus died after holding his
miserable office for only three years and was succeeded by a
certain Timaeus who appeared to be doomed to an equally
degraded impotence.

But as it happened the days of Paul were numbered. In the
autumn of 271 Aurelian, who had become the Roman
Emperor, turned his arms against Zenobia. He seized Antioch,
he inflicted a severe defeat on the Queen, and possessed himself
of her person and her capital. Paul had now no political
support, and was doubtless known to the Emperor for his anti-
Roman proclivities. The hour of the orthodox church had
come. They appealed for help to Aurelian; and though this
appeal of the Christian Church to a heathen might be considered somewhat unscrupulous, it was successful. Aurelian
ordered Paul to leave Antioch and decreed that the church
buildings and estates should be delivered to the person designated
by the bishop of Rome. What would Firmilian have thought
of such proceedings? In any case Firmilian was dead. The
bishop of Rome handed over the property of the church to the
delighted Timaeus and the triumph of orthodoxy was complete. Whether Paul had feathered his nest sufficiently to be
able to retire in comfort we do not know. He vanishes completely from history. The time and manner of his death are
never mentioned. Only his name remained for many years
as that of an arch-heretic, and even his name has now been
forgotten except by curious students of ecclesiastical history.

Methodius

Little is known about the life of Methodius. Was he
bishop, simultaneously, of Olympus and Patara? Was he,
against the canons of the Church, translated to the see of
Tyre? Was he martyred by Decius, Valerian or Diocletian?

And was the place of his martyrdom Chalcis in Greece, or Chalchis in Syria? The answers to these important questions are concealed by the mist of time. Of the writings of Methodius, most of which have disappeared, we will only consider the *Banquet of the Ten Virgins, a Dialogue Concerning Chastity*.

Methodius perhaps thought his *Banquet* was an answer to the *Banquet* of Plato. A nineteenth-century theologian says it presents "a contrast as strong as possible between the swinish sensuality of false 'philosophy' in its best estate and the heavenly chastity of those whom the Gospel declares 'they shall see God'." Unfortunately the contrast is as strong as possible in other ways. It is best to forget altogether the beauty and nobility of Plato while dipping into the pages of Methodius. In the usual fashion of the early Fathers he takes passage after passage of the Old Testament, and by an allegorical interpretation proves that they were all written to exalt virginity. When the Psalmist says, "As for our harps we hanged them up upon the willows beside the river", he is "clearly giving the name of harps to their bodies which they hung upon the branches of chastity, fastening them to the wood that they might not be snatched away and dragged off by the stream of incontinence". When Jeremiah says, "A maid should not forget her ornaments nor a bride her attire", he shows "she should not give up or loosen the band of chastity through wiles and distraction". The whole of the delicious love poem, the *Song of Solomon*, is really a song in praise of virginity. "Thou hast ravished my heart, my sister, my spouse," means "By the most lovely sight of thy mind thou hast urged my heart to love, radiating forth from within the glorious beauty of chastity."

Methodius is very fond of the agnos tree. Liddell and Scott tell us it is a tall tree like the willow, the branches of which were strewn by matrons on their beds at the festival of Thesmophoria. It was associated with the notion of chastity from the likeness of its name to *agnus*, and is sometimes called *vitex agnuscastus*. It is a bit awkward that the Thesmophoria was in reality a festival in honour of the corn goddess, and the rites performed exclusively by women at that time were "for the purpose of quickening the ground and the wombs of women". Perhaps Methodius cannot be expected to know this; in any case he firmly calls it the tree of chastity. For some unknown reason he says it is the same tree as the bramble, and recounting the parable of the trees from the ninth chapter of Judges in which the trees agree together to make the bramble their king, he affirms that this foretells the future reign of chastity. Unfortunately this makes complete nonsense of the parable, in which the bramble stands for the wicked King Abimelech—fire bursting from the bramble burns up both the shameless ones who made him king and the king-bramble itself. Methodius tries again with the story of Elijah who "fleeing from the face of the woman Jezebel at first came under a bramble, and there . . . received strength and took food; signifying that to him who flies from the incitements of lust, and from a woman —that is, from pleasure—the tree of chastity is a refuge and a shade". Methodius might have done well to act on the words he puts into the mouth of the virgin Thaleia: "It is a dangerous thing wholly to despise the literal meaning."

The virgins of the Banquet, like those of the Shepherd of Hermas, may seem to us somewhat equivocal in their language. Domnina tells us that "the devil, having beguiled the man by its imitations, led him captive, persuading him to conceal the nakedness of his body by fig-leaves." This might seem an example of proper decency with which we should hardly credit the devil. Domnina sees further. In fact, she continues, "by their friction he incited him to sexual pleasure." Theophila is much concerned with "the embraces of connubial love", and throws out an interesting piece of physiological information. "The marrow-like and generative part of the blood," she tells us, "like a kind of liquid bone, coming together from all the members, worked into foam and curdled, is projected through the organs of generation into the living body of the female." We should hardly have expected a virgin to be so well informed.

It has been supposed that the *Banquet* was aimed at Origen, who, we have already pointed out, is rebuked for over-allegorising. At the end the real cause of Methodius's antagonism comes out.

"Shall we not say that the soul which is deluged with the surging waves of passion and yet does not on that account weary or grow faint, but directs her vessel—that is, the flesh—nobly into the port of chastity, is better and more estimable than he that navigates in calm weather? . . . Therefore the soul that is concupiscent and exercises self-control . . . is better than one that is not concupiscent."

Thus Methodius puts Origen in his place.

VI

The Last Persecution

HE persecution of Valerian in which Dionysius was
banished and Cyprian killed was followed by thirty
years of peace. Then came the terrible persecution to
which the name of Diocletian has been, somewhat unjustly,
attached. It is true that it started while Diocletian was Emperor,
but it was only set in motion by the machinations of the
Caesar, Galerius. It began in 303, with the destruction of
churches and Christian writings, and rapidly developed into a
general attack on all believers. In the West, the attitude of the
authorities was much milder, and in 305 the persecution there
petered out altogether. In that year Diocletian abdicated
and his place was taken by the ruthless Galerius. In the East,
therefore, the ill-treatment of the Christians continued, ebbing
and flowing in violence for many years. In 310 Galerius
developed a painful and malignant disease. In his agony he
turned to those he had been attacking for so long, and in
return for relaxing his cruelties, begged them to pray to their
god on his behalf. These prayers, which, if offered, we can
hardly believe were very ardent, proved unavailing. Galerius
died in 311 and was succeeded by Maximin, who renewed the
persecution, with horrible cruelties; all the East suffered in
unspeakable ways. Shortly afterwards, however, things began
to take a more hopeful turn. Constantine was gaining power
in the West. He was favourable to Christianity, and attempted
to curb the monstrosities Maximin was committing. In 312
he defeated the usurper Maxentius at the battle of the Milvian
Bridge, where he saw the cross in the sky with the words, "In
this sign conquer" flaming above it. At the same time he discovered that Maximin had been secretly leagued with Maxentius. This proved the doom of Maximin. In the following

year he was defeated by Licinius, Constantine's colleague, and shortly afterwards committed suicide. Licinius and Constantine now met at Milan, and together promulgated the famous Edict of Milan, extending toleration of all religions to all parts of the Empire. The struggle was, however, not yet over. Licinius began to turn against Constantine and at the same time more or less overtly against the Christians. His enmity towards them increased month by month. They were dismissed from their offices, their goods were confiscated, they were exiled, condemned to the mines, sold into slavery. Not a few suffered death and the terror was mounting. But the end was in sight. The friction between Licinius and Constantine led to an outbreak of hostilities between them, and Licinius was defeated in two battles. He was sent under guard to Thessalonica where he appears to have started intriguing once more. In any case the soldiers demanded his death and he was executed in 323. Constantine was now sole Emperor. The persecutions of the Christians by the heathens were over for sixteen hundred years.

During the period we have so briefly covered there are two writers who claim our attention—Arnobius and Lactantius.

Arnobius

Arnobius, like Tertullian and Cyprian, was an inhabitant of North Africa and wrote in Latin. The little we know of him personally comes from Jerome, who tells us that he was a successful teacher of rhetoric at Sicca in Africa in the reign of Diocletian. He himself tells us that he was a heathen in his youth. "But lately," he writes, "O blindness, I worshipped images just brought from the furnaces, gods made on anvils and forged with hammers, the bones of elephants, paintings, wreaths on aged trees; whenever I espied an anointed stone, one bedaubed with olive oil, . . . I worshipped it, I addressed myself to it and begged blessings from a senseless block. . . .

But now, having been led into the paths of truth by so great a teacher, I know what all these things are."

Jerome says that Arnobius "was brought to the faith by a vision; and not being received by the bishop, for he had been a persistent enemy of Christ, composed very excellent books against his former belief". It seems improbable that his extant work *Against the Heathen* can be what Jerome is alluding to; it is very long, in seven books, and its writing almost certainly occupied several years. Moreover the doctrine it contains would have been unlikely to have pleased his bishop. He maintains that God did not create the souls of men, his doctrine of Christ is undoubtedly heretical, and he declares that it is a great error to speak or even to think about the nature of God. "There is but one thing man can be assured of, regarding God's nature; to know and perceive that nothing can be revealed in human language concerning God." Arnobius may be right; but it is unlikely that the dignitaries of the Church who spent their lives in arguing about the Trinity, the Incarnation and the Procession of the Holy Ghost, would feel much sympathy with these views.

It appears probable from internal evidence that the various books were written at different times. In the second book, after stating that nothing can be *proved* about the future, he goes on, "Is it not more rational, of two things uncertain and hanging in doubtful suspense, rather to believe what carries with it some hopes, than what brings none at all? For in the one case there is no danger . . . in the other there is the greatest loss, even the loss of salvation. . . ." This is a thought which we know from the famous *wager* of Pascal (1623–1662).

"S'il y a un Dieu il est infiniment incompréhensible. . . . Nous sommes donc incapables de connaître ni ce qu'il est, ni s'il est. . . . Oui, mais il faut parier: cela n'est pas volontaire, vous êtes embarqué. . . . Estimons ces deux cas: si vous gagnez vous gagnez tout: si vous perdez vous ne perdez rien." ("If God exists he is infinitely incomprehensible. . . . We are therefore incapable of knowing what he is or whether he is. . . . Yes, but you must wager on it: you have no choice, you are already involved. . . . Consider the two cases: if you win you win everything: if you lose you lose nothing.") *Pensées* 223.

In France, in the reign of Louis XIV there was, it is true, no danger in being a Christian, you lost nothing by betting that God existed; but in the Roman Empire in the days of Diocletian it was far otherwise. Arnobius must surely have written these words before A.D. 303. Other passages were certainly later. "What do you say, you who urge us to worship your gods by the fear of bodily tortures?" "Why have our writings deserved to be given up to the flames and our meetings cruelly broken up?" This destruction of the Christian scriptures was precisely what was ordered by Diocletian's first edict of 303; the "bodily tortures" were to follow all too soon.

It would not indeed be surprising if Arnobius's own book had been condemned to be burnt, for his attack on the heathen gods is outspoken and virulent. Like Tertullian and Clement of Alexandria whom he quotes freely, he has gathered together a vast collection of fantastic and scurrilous tales of Greek and Roman mythology—a collection which, like theirs, has proved an astonishing storehouse for modern students of these subjects.

We may perhaps close our account of Arnobius with some of the address he supposes an ox, selected as a sacrificial victim, to make to Jupiter.

"Is this then, O Jupiter, or whatever god you are, is this humane or right, or should it be considered at all just, that when another has sinned I should be killed? Ought you to allow satisfaction to be made to you by my blood, although I never did you wrong, never wittingly or unwittingly did violence to your divinity and majesty? I am, as you know, a dumb animal, simple in my nature, not given to be fickle in my manners. Did I ever celebrate your games with too little reverence? . . . Did I ever swear falsely by your name? Did I

sacrilegiously steal your property and plunder your temples?
. . . What then is the reason that the crime of another is
atoned for by my blood, and that my life and innocence
are made to pay for wickedness with which I have nothing
to do?"

The unfortunate ox who makes this pathetic appeal had,
it is evident, never heard of the doctrine of Vicarious Suffering.

Lactantius

Lactantius was a pupil of Arnobius. Like him he was in early
life a pagan and teacher of rhetoric, and may have been a
native of Africa. His reputation was so great that the Emperor
Diocletian summoned him to Nicomedia to teach rhetoric
there. It was probably during his stay in Nicomedia that he
was converted to Christianity and doubtless lost his post when
the persecution began in A.D. 303. He was thus reduced to
extreme poverty and probably occupied his enforced leisure
with literary work. His specifically religious writings are
The Divine Institutions and *The Wrath of God*. He also wrote
The Workmanship of God, in reality a treatise on physiology, and
The Deaths of Persecutors, a historical narrative, dealing princip-
ally with the period from the outbreak of Diocletian's persecution to the Edict of Milan in A.D. 313. Its object is to prove the
truth of Christianity by the horrible deaths which overtook
those who persecuted the Church.

Shortly after the Empire was divided between Constantine
and Licinius, Lactantius's position took a turn for the better.
Though he was by now advanced in years Constantine summoned him to Gaul and made him tutor to his son Crispus. He
seems to have remained there peacefully till his death, which
is thought to have taken place at Treves, towards 325.

The Workmanship of God is especially interesting as showing
what was known or guessed about the functioning of the
human body at the beginning of the fourth century. Much of

this knowledge must derive from Galen (*c.* 200), whom, however, he never mentions—but Lactantius naturally gives a religious twist to his facts. He attributes much of the outward formation of the body to God's desire to give men a beautiful appearance. The eyebrows, for instance, are ornamental. "How beautiful the other parts are can scarcely be expressed—the chin, gently drawn down from the cheeks, and the lower part of it so closed that the lightly imprinted division appears to mark its extreme point; the neck stiff and well rounded; . . . the upper arms standing out with remarkable muscles; the useful and becoming bending of the elbows." In describing the hand he notes the importance of the thumb being opposed to the other fingers, and adds, "It has two joints . . . not as the others, three; but one is attached to the hand for the sake of beauty, for if it had had three joints and been separated the foul and unbecoming appearance would have deprived the hand of all grace." "The toes are of the same number as the fingers, for the sake of appearance, rather than utility." The nose has been contrived "so that it should not deform the beauty of the face, which would certainly have been the case if there had been only one single aperture". As regards the nose he further observes that "the lower part has a soft cartilege attached to it that it may be pliant to the use of the fingers." May we suppose that Lactantius is here alluding to the act of blowing the nose? In this connexion it may be pointed out that his teacher, Arnobius, is the first writer to use a word meaning "handkerchief"—"muccinium".

He has observed that deafness and dumbness go together, but curiously imagines that deafness is caused by dumbness.

He is unable to explain the use of most of the internal organs —the kidneys, the spleen, the liver—of what use are they? "Some say that the amorous passions are contained in the liver." Where is the mind located? In the head or the breast or in the blood contained in the heart? Or, having no fixed locality, does it run here and there, scattered through the whole body? He enquires also into the nature of the soul, which he considers to be part of the body. It is certainly immortal, as it cannot be seen or touched, but is it the same as the mind? It is all a mystery. We may, however, arrive at one conclusion. "Whoever measures man by his flesh is in error. For this wretched little body with which we are clothed is but the receptacle of man. . . . And if he shall be more luxurious and delicate in his life than nature demands . . . he shall fall and be pressed down to the earth; but if he shall do his duty . . . and constantly maintain his position . . . if he shall not allow himself to be enslaved to the earth, which he ought to trample on and overcome, he will gain eternal life."

The Divine Institutions is a defence of Christianity. Lactantius writes, he tells us, to supplement the writings of Tertullian and Cyprian—he controverts not only the mythology but the philosophy of the heathens. Socrates, Plato, Aristotle and many lesser thinkers, have their folly and wickedness exposed. Even Cicero, most eloquent of men, was generally wrong. Christianity confutes them all. Having dealt with the great thinkers of the past, he turns to two of his contemporaries.

"When I was teaching rhetoric in Bithynia," he says, ". . . at the time when the temple of God was thrown down, there were living at the same place two men who insulted the truth as it lay prostrate and overthrown, I know not whether with greater arrogance or harshness." They are neither of them named, but one of them has been identified as Hierocles, the governor of Bithynia and promoter of the great persecution, who under the name of Philalethes—the Friend of Truth— wrote a treatise *To the Christians*. According to Lactantius he had been a believer, but had apostatised from the faith. He certainly appears to have had considerable knowledge of the Christian religion, but he probably stole most of it from the writings of Porphyry (233–304). He has a curious story, the source of which is quite unknown. He declares that Jesus, after being driven away by the Jews, put himself at the head of a band of nine hundred brigands, with whom he ravaged Palestine. It was for this criminal behaviour that he was crucified.

Of his other opponent, Lactantius says, "He was so addicted to vice, that though a teacher of abstinence he was not less inflamed by avarice than by lusts. He was so extravagant in his manner of living that though in his school he supported virtue and praised parsimony and poverty, he dined less sumptuously in a palace than at his own house." He showed his claims to philosophy by wearing a long beard and the philosopher's cloak—these, says Lactantius, "sheltered his vices", which were also concealed by the greatest veil of all—wealth. He used his money to bribe judges and "make a traffic of their decisions". "This man . . . vomited forth three books against the Christian religion and name. . . . And he broke out profusely into praise of the princes whose piety and foresight, he said, had been distinguished . . . in defending the religious rites of the gods." "Everyone, however, blamed him for undertaking this work at the very time when odious cruelty raged. O philosopher! a flatterer and a time-server! But this man was despised, as his vanity deserved: for he did not gain the popularity which he hoped for, and the glory which he eagerly sought for was changed to censure and blame."

Thus once more the machinations of the Evil One were brought to nothing.

The Divine Institutions, dedicated to Constantine the Great, and written not many years before the official recognition of Christianity in the Empire, is the last of the great Apologies against the heathens.

The first epoch of Church History ends. The next epoch— that of the great Church Councils—is inaugurated by the Council of Nicea A.D. 325 in which the Nicene Creed is formulated. Henceforward, the battle against heathen persecutors having been won, the combative efforts of the Fathers are directed against their Christian enemies—the heretics.

Authors *in italics* wrote in Latin. The rest in Greek.
P marks the persecuting Emperors.
† marks the date of death.

Emperors

P 81 Domitian   Clement of Rome 95
    96 Nerva
P 98 Trajan   Papias *fl.* 100
                            Ignatius *c.* 110

   117 Hadrian
   138 Antoninus Pius

                            Shepherd of Hermas
                            Epistle of Barnabas before 150
                            Martyrdom of Polycarp 155
P 161 Marcus Aurelius

                            Justin Martyr martyred 165
                            Tatian *fl.* 170
                            Irenaeus *fl.* 177
   180 Commodus   Narcissus B. of Jerusalem 180
                            Theophilus of Antioch † 181
                                              Minucius Felix?

   193 Septimus Severus
   211 Caracalla, Geta
                            Clement of Alexandria *fl.* 190–210
   218 Elagabalus   *Tertullian*
   222 Alexander   *fl.* 200–220
P 235 Maximin   Hippolytus † 236
   238 Gordian III   Julius Africanus † 240
   243 Philip
P 249 Decius   *Novatian fl.* 250
                                              Commodianus
                                              fl. 250

P 254 Valerian   Origen † 254

                                              Cyprian
                                              Martyred 259

Authors *in italics* wrote in Latin. The rest in Greek.

P marks the persecuting Emperors.

† marks the date of death.

Emperors

Gallienus	Dionysius of Alexandria † 265
270 Aurelian	Paul of Samosata *fl.* 265
	Gregory Thaumaturge † 272
P 284 Diocletian	Methodius † 311? *Arnobius fl.* 284
	Lactantius fl. 300
313 Edict of Milan	
323 Constantine the	
Great sole	
Emperor	

Translations of all the Fathers quoted will be found in the Ante-Nicene Library, published in America 1887. Individual writings are to be found in various collections, among which mention may be made of the publications of the Society for Promoting Christian Knowledge. The *Ecclesisatical History* of Eusebius (*c.* 260–340), translated in the Loeb Library (pub. Heinemann, 1920), contains many fragments which have not been preserved elsewhere. The apocryphal writings will be found in M. R. James' *Apocrypha of the New Testament* (pub. Clarendon Press, 1924).

A very good short account of the subject will be found in H. B. Swete's *Patristic Study* (pub. 1902). The best history of the period in a moderate compass is Monsignor Duchesne's *Early History of the Christian Church to the end of the Fifth Century* (pub. Paris, 1908–1918). This learned work is comprehensive and broadminded, and written with so much wit and humour that it makes delightful reading. It was, however, placed on the Index of Prohibited Books in 1913, where it still remains.

The questions raised by the letter of Abgar are fully discussed by J. Rendel Harris in *The Dioscuri in Christian Legends* (London & Cambridge University Press, 1903) and *The Cult of the Heavenly Twins* (C.U.P., 1906).

The date and character of the story of Paul and Thecla in the apocryphal Acts of Paul is investigated by Sir William Ramsay in the *Church in the Roman Empire* (Hodder & Stoughton, 1903) and by S. Reinach in *Cultes, Mythes et Religions*, vol. 5 (Paris, 1923).